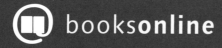

Read this book online today:

With SAP PRESS BooksOnline we offer you online access to knowledge from the leading SAP experts. Whether you use it as a beneficial supplement or as an alternative to the printed book, with SAP PRESS BooksOnline you can:

- Access your book anywhere, at any time. All you need is an Internet connection.
- Perform full text searches on your book and on the entire SAP PRESS library.
- Build your own personalized SAP library.

The SAP PRESS customer advantage:

Register this book today at *www.sap-press.com* and obtain exclusive free trial access to its online version. If you like it (and we think you will), you can choose to purchase permanent, unrestricted access to the online edition at a very special price!

Here's how to get started:

1. Visit *www.sap-press.com*.
2. Click on the link for SAP PRESS BooksOnline and login (or create an account).
3. Enter your free trial license key, shown below in the corner of the page.
4. Try out your online book with full, unrestricted access for a limited time!

Your personal free trial **license key** for this online book is:

fivd-6t25-jm4s-r7eq

100 Things You Should Know About HR Management with SAP®

 PRESS

SAP PRESS is a joint initiative of SAP and Galileo Press. The know-how offered by SAP specialists combined with the expertise of the Galileo Press publishing house offers the reader expert books in the field. SAP PRESS features first-hand information and expert advice, and provides useful skills for professional decision-making.

SAP PRESS offers a variety of books on technical and business related topics for the SAP user. For further information, please visit our website: www.sap-press.com.

Greg Newman
Discover SAP ERP HCM
2009, 438 pp.
978-1-59229-222-6

Martin Gillet
Configuring and Customizing Employee and Manager Self-Services in SAP ERP HCM
2011, 400 pp.
978-1-59229-356-8

Masters, Kotsakis, Krishnamoorthy
E-Recruiting with SAP ERP HCM
2010, 358 pp.
978-1-59229-243-1

Masters and Kotsakis
Enterprise Compensation Management with SAP ERP HCM
2009, 405 pp.
978-1-59229-207-3

Ajay Jain Bhutoria and Cameron Lewis

100 Things You Should Know About
HR Management with SAP®

Bonn • Boston

Galileo Press is named after the Italian physicist, mathematician and philosopher Galileo Galilei (1564–1642). He is known as one of the founders of modern science and an advocate of our contemporary, heliocentric worldview. His words *Eppur se muove* (And yet it moves) have become legendary. The Galileo Press logo depicts Jupiter orbited by the four Galilean moons, which were discovered by Galileo in 1610.

Editor Meg Dunkerley
Copyeditor Mike Beady
Cover Design Graham Geary
Photo Credit iStockphoto.com/peepo
Layout Design Graham Geary
Production Manager Kelly O'Callaghan
Assistant Production Editor Graham Geary
Typesetting Publishers' Design and Production Services, Inc.
Printed and bound in Canada

ISBN 978-1-59229-361-2

© 2011 by Galileo Press Inc., Boston (MA)
1st Edition 2011

Library of Congress Cataloging-in-Publication Data
Bhutoria, Ajay Jain.
  100 things you should know about HR Management with SAP / Ajay Jain Bhutoria, Cameron Lewis. — 1st ed.
    p. cm.
  ISBN-13: 978-1-59229-361-2
  ISBN-10: 1-59229-361-1
  1. SAP ERP. 2. Personnel management—Computer programs. I. Lewis, Cameron. II. Title. III. Title: One hundred things you should know about HR Management with SAP.
    HF5549.5.D37B37 2011
    658.300285'53—dc22
                                  2010036292

All rights reserved. Neither this publication nor any part of it may be copied or reproduced in any form or by any means or translated into another language, without the prior consent of Galileo Press GmbH, Rheinwerkallee 4, 53227 Bonn, Germany.

Galileo Press makes no warranties or representations with respect to the content hereof and specifically disclaims any implied warranties of merchantability or fitness for any particular purpose. Galileo Press assumes no responsibility for any errors that may appear in this publication.

"Galileo Press" and the Galileo Press logo are registered trademarks of Galileo Press GmbH, Bonn, Germany. SAP PRESS is an imprint of Galileo Press.

All of the screenshots and graphics reproduced in this book are subject to copyright © SAP AG, Dietmar-Hopp-Allee 16, 69190 Walldorf, Germany.

SAP, the SAP-Logo, mySAP, mySAP.com, mySAP Business Suite, SAP NetWeaver, SAP R/3, SAP R/2, SAP B2B, SAPtronic, SAPscript, SAP BW, SAP CRM, SAP Early Watch, SAP ArchiveLink, SAP GUI, SAP Business Workflow, SAP Business Engineer, SAP Business Navigator, SAP Business Framework, SAP Business Information Warehouse, SAP inter-enterprise solutions, SAP APO, AcceleratedSAP, InterSAP, SAPoffice, SAPfind, SAPfile, SAPtime, SAPmail, SAPaccess, SAP-EDI, R/3 Retail, Accelerated HR, Accelerated HiTech, Accelerated Consumer Products, ABAP, ABAP/4, ALE/WEB, Alloy, BAPI, Business Framework, BW Explorer, Duet, Enjoy-SAP, mySAP.com e-business platform, mySAP Enterprise Portals, RIVA, SAPPHIRE, TeamSAP, Webflow and SAP PRESS are registered or unregistered trademarks of SAP AG, Walldorf, Germany.

All other products mentioned in this book are registered or unregistered trademarks of their respective companies.

Contents at a Glance

1	Personnel Administration	16
2	Organizational Management	32
3	Benefits	48
4	Payroll	64
5	Time Management	90
6	E-Recruiting	120
7	Performance Management	132
8	Compensation Management	148
9	Career Succession and Planning	178
10	Employee Self-Service and Manager Self-Service	186
11	Adobe Forms and Processes	216
12	HR Administrator Role	230
13	HR Security Authorization Management	240
14	Reporting	250
15	Miscellaneous	270

Dear Reader,

Have you ever spent days trying to figure out how to generate a personnel report in SAP ERP HCM only to find out you just needed to click a few buttons? If so, you'll be delighted with this book — it unlocks the secrets of SAP ERP HCM. It provides users and super-users with 100 tips and workarounds you can use to increase productivity, save time, and improve the overall ease-of-use of SAP ERP HCM. The tips have been carefully selected to provide a collection of the best, most useful, and rarest information.

Thanks to the hard work and dedication of Ajay Jain Bhutoria and Cameron Lewis, reading this book will put you in the best possible position to maximize your time and make your job easier. Throughout the course of writing the manuscript, the authors continually impressed me with their dedication to this work. You are now the recipient of this knowledge and dedication, and I'm confident that you'll benefit greatly from both.

We appreciate your business, and welcome your feedback. Your comments and suggestions are the most useful tools to help us improve our books for you, the reader. We encourage you to visit our website at *www.sap-press.com* and share your feedback about this work.

Thank you for purchasing a book from SAP PRESS!

Meg Dunkerley
Editor, SAP PRESS

Galileo Press
100 Grossman Drive, Suite 205
Braintree, MA 02184

meg.dunkerley@galileo-press.com
www.sap-press.com

Contents

Acknowledgments 13
Introduction 14

PART 1 Personnel Administration 16
    1   Deleting a Personnel Number in SAP ERP HCM 18
    2   Fast Entry to Maintain Master Data 20
    3   Changing the Entry or Leaving Date 22
    4   Tracking Logged Changes in Infotype PA 24
    5   Finding the Personnel Number Using Quick Search Tips 26
    6   Creating a Personnel Administration Custom Infotype 28
    7   Fast Entry of Personnel Actions 30

PART 2 Organizational Management 32
    8   Simplifying Organizational Management Maintenance 34
    9   Generating a List of Features Easily 36
    10   Tracking Logged Changes to Organizational Management Data 38
    11   Vacancy Tracking in Organizational Management 40
    12   Maintaining Vacancy of Positions 42
    13   Adding a Customer-Specific Field to a Personnel Development Infotype 44
    14   Searching People and Organizational Management Objects Easily 46

PART 3 Benefits 48
    15   Changing Employee Benefits Using Adjustment Reasons 50
    16   Hide-Optional Fields on Benefits Infotypes 52
    17   Using the Benefits Toolset Plan Cost Summary Report 54
    18   Creating a New Benefit Plan Faster by Copying an Existing Plan 56
    19   Overriding the Benefit Salary on Life Insurance 58
    20   Controlling Open Enrollment with an Adjustment Reason ... 60

Contents

	21	Managing Year-End Adjustment Payroll Runs for Terminated Employees	62

PART 4 Payroll — 64

	22	Deleting Old Payroll Processes	66
	23	Changing the Earliest Retro-Accounting Date/Master Data Change on Payroll Status	68
	24	Reversing Your Posting Run Documents	70
	25	Auditing Payroll and Time Schema with Subschemas and PCRs	72
	26	Displaying Deleted Payroll Results	74
	27	Inserting Custom Messages in Employee Pay Stubs	76
	28	Performing Special and Year-End Adjustments for Payroll	80
	29	Updating Payroll Schemas and PCRs with Line Editor Commands	82
	30	Creating Files for Third Party Providers	84
	31	Deleting Current Payroll Results for an Employee	88

PART 5 Time Management — 90

	32	Using Report RPUSWH00 for Infotype 0007 — Mass Update	92
	33	Troubleshooting Payroll and Time-Related Issues and Displaying Time Evaluation Results	96
	34	Generating Automatic Absence Quotas	100
	35	Checking Attendance and Absence Types	102
	36	Displaying the Personnel Work Schedule for Multiple Employees for a Given Period	106
	37	Displaying and Changing Your Holiday Calendar	110
	38	Simplifying Your SAP Time Evaluation Schema	114
	39	Reviewing the Error Log Generated During Time Evaluation	116
	40	Correcting Absence Quotas Generated in Time Evaluation	118

PART 6 E-Recruiting — 120

	41	Using the Recruiter's Work Center Dashboard to Manage Your Requisitions and Applications	122
	42	Conducting Efficient Background Checks	124

	43	Managing Your Recruiting Administration Activities with the Recruiting Administrator Role	126
	44	Managing Performance Management Functions and Reporting via One Transaction	130

PART 7 Performance Management ... 132

	45	Evaluating Appraisal Results, Creating Ranking Lists, and Comparing Appraisal Documents	134
	46	Changing Your Appraisal Document	138
	47	Changing the Customizing Settings for Your Appraisals	142
	48	Controlling Access to Training Courses in the SAP Learning Solution	144
	49	Managing Your Backend Objective Setting and Appraisal Process	146

PART 8 Compensation Management ... 148

	50	Designing a Salary Increase Program on a Single Worksheet	150
	51	Adding or Changing the Layout of Compensation Planning Worksheets	154
	52	Tracking and Monitoring Compensation Planning Changes	156
	53	Notifying the Planning Manager to Start Compensation Planning	158
	54	Managing and Monitoring your Compensation Budget Reconciliation through the Planning Cycle	160
	55	Deleting Sensitive Compensation Planning History Data from the Test Environment	162
	56	Controlling Exceptions on Eligibility for Compensation Plans	164
	57	Mass Updating Basic Pay Based on Changes during Compensation Planning and Review for Changes	166
	58	Managing Compensation Administration Activities via Compensation Specialist Roles in the Portal	168
	59	Customizing the MSS ECM Screen Layout to Hide Unnecessary Columns	172
	60	Adjusting Your Compensation Process Records	174
	61	Renaming Column Headers in the MSS–ECM Compensation Planning Worksheet	176

PART 9 Career Succession and Planning 178

- 62 Comparing Talent Profiles Using the Compare Functionality 180
- 63 Using Succession Planning to Organize Your Processes 182
- 64 Designing Your Job Architecture for Efficient Succession Planning 184

PART 10 Employee Self-Service and Manager Self-Service 186

- 65 Displaying Table Contents for Master Data Fields 188
- 66 Control Settings for Subtype Display on ESS 190
- 67 Personalizing Your Workflow Task List Display Page 192
- 68 Control the Visibility of Personal Information Fields on Employee Self-Service (ESS) Screens 196
- 69 Multiple Ways You Can Search for Employees in Manager Self-Service (MSS) 198
- 70 Launching Manager's Desk Top Reports from the Launch Pad in MSS 202
- 71 Setting the Approval Working Time in MSS Using the Collective Approval Screen 204
- 72 Controlling Absence and Attendance Types Displayed in Multiple iViews in ESS 206
- 73 Using Guided Procedures to Streamline the User Experience for Benefits Enrollment and Life and Work Events in ESS 208
- 74 Controlling Personnel Information Infotypes for Employees 212
- 75 Customizing Your System Messages on Employee Self-Service 214

PART 11 Adobe Forms and Processes 216

- 76 Managing the Hire-to-Terminate Employee Lifecycle Using SAP HCM Forms and Processes in MSS 218
- 77 HCM Forms and Process Architecture 222
- 78 Processing Multiple Employee's Records in Processes and Forms 226
- 79 Defining the Attachment Types Required for Your Form Scenario 228

PART 12 HR Administrator Role **230**

80	Running a Free Text Search	232
81	Editing Employee Data in MSS from the Work Center	234
82	Using the Digital Personnel File to Simplify and Optimize HR Administrator	236
83	Using the HR Administrator Role for All Administrative HR Tasks	238

PART 13 HR Security Authorization Management **240**

84	Controlling Employee Access to Self-Service Capabilities	242
85	Restricting Users from Viewing or Maintaining Their Own SAP ERP HCM Master Data	244
86	Accessing Users' SU53 Transaction from Your Own Desktop	246
87	Checking the Integrity of Data Entered in SAP ERP HCM	248

PART 14 Reporting **250**

88	Comparing Two Security Roles to Maintain Your Authorizations and SOX Compliance	252
89	Improving the Performance of Your Reports and Queries Using Dynamic Selections	254
90	Executing Reports from the MSS Launch Pad	258
91	Executing HR Reports Using Structural Display	260
92	Using QuickViewer to Create Basic List Reports for Occasional HR and Payroll Users	262
93	Transporting Reports Developed in the SAP Query Standard Area from One System to Another	266

PART 15 Miscellaneous **270**

94	Translating Your Organizational Structure into Multiple Languages	272
95	Creating Standard and Structural Authorization Profiles and Roles	274
96	Displaying Long Text on Infotypes	276
97	Transporting Your Organizational Structure Manually	278
98	Using Transaction Codes to Access HR IMG Nodes	280

	99	Creating Custom Transaction Codes for Your Day-to-Day HR Activities 282
	100	Creating a Mini Information Board on the SAP GUI Log-On Screen 284

Additional Resources 286
The Authors 292
Index 293

Acknowledgments

I wish to thank my parents, sons Raj and Yash, and a special thank you to my wife Vinita — your dedication and support in making sure I finally finished this effort turned a possibility into a reality.

I would also like to thank Vijay Bhutoria, Sr. Human Capital Management Consultant for his valued knowledge and contributions in putting together technical and functional details for various tips in this book.

I would also like to thank SAP Help and SAP Release Documents that I used for validation and cross checks.

Last, but not least, I would like to thank my best friend and co-author Cameron Lewis for spending weeks and weeks with me in putting together this book. For sure without your support and dedication this book would not be possible today.

I would also like to thank Meg Dunkerley and the entire Galileo Press team for their support and cooperation.

Ajay Jain Bhutoria

I'd like to thank my wife Debbie for a marriage full of laughs, hope and inspiration… and my sons Tyler and Ian for their wit and sense of humor. You all have helped me stay young.

I'd also like to thank my dear friend and co-author Ajay Jain Bhutoria for including me in this journey through SAP ERP HCM. It's been quite an adventure.

Cameron Lewis

Introduction

This book is one of the first of a new series of SAP ERP books based on 100 ideas for various SAP software components. It is designed to make reading and understanding SAP ERP more interesting and accessible for your day to day work. You can flip through this book and search for ideas on each page to see if any of the 100 topics catches your attention. If so, you can read through the idea in a matter of minutes and decide whether you'd like to research the topic further. Most ideas are two pages long so you can see the entire idea on each open page. Since its limited how much information can be placed on two pages, each idea generally references other materials where you can do further research and reading.

SAP ERP Human Capital Management (SAP ERP HCM) is a global, integrated human resources management solution that helps executives, human resources (HR) professionals, and line-of-business (LOB) leaders to hire talent; manage, cultivate, and reward employees; and align employee goals with business objectives.

If you are currently using SAP ERP HCM, this is the resource you need. This book was written to help you, the everyday user in HR and IT, tap into the wisdom of SAP experts and the secrets of the SAP system to build your knowledge and increase your productivity. It is a collection of the best, most useful and perhaps least well-known tips that cover time-saving shortcuts and workarounds. These 100 tips will help you get the most out of your daily interaction with the system.

The book is broken down into 12 different parts, with relevant tips within each. Each tip was created for one of those "Aha!" moments – which provides you with the information you didn't even know you needed. Topic highlights include the following:

- **Process Management**
    - Daily or routine personnel administration tasks
    - OM data administration
    - Benefits process and data administration
    - Payroll administration
    - Time management processes and data administration

- **Talent Management**
  - Staffing processes
  - Performance management processes and data administration
  - Compensation management processes and data administration
  - Career succession and planning processes and data management
- **End-User Services**
  - ESS and MSS processes and data management
  - Adobe process and forms framework
  - HR Administrator role
  - Security authorization management
  - SAP reporting tools and capabilities.
- **Miscellaneous**
  - Translations
  - Long text
  - Transporting org structures, relationships, and objects
  - Saving transaction codes as favorites
  - Customizing the SAP logon screen
  - Using SE16 to assign custom transaction codes to tables or reports

We hope this book brings you the insight and clarity you didn't realize you needed. You can read it from cover to cover, or jump around between tips. Either way, we hope we have provided you with the valuable resource you are looking for.

Part 1
Personnel Administration

Things You'll Learn in this Section
1. Deleting a Personnel Number in SAP ERP HCM 18
2. Fast Entry to Maintain Master Data 20
3. Changing the Entry or Leaving Date 22
4. Tracking Logged Changes in Infotype PA 24
5. Finding the Personnel Number Using Quick Search Tips 26
6. Creating a Personnel Administration Custom Infotype 28
7. Fast Entry of Personnel Actions 30

In times when company resources are constrained, the operational efficiency and effectiveness becomes a priority for every organization. The efficient administration of personnel data is a decisive advantage. This section of tips will help developers, business analysts, system administrators, and functional power-users in HR and IT manage the daily or routine personnel administration tasks in SAP ERP HCM, saving time and money for more strategic activities. Topics covered include HR infotypes, reports, standard utility, fast entry, and quick search functionalities.

Tip 1: Deleting a Personnel Number in SAP ERP HCM

You can use the standard utility functionality to remove extraneous personnel numbers from the system.

After a candidate accepts a job offer, you can use the prehire action in SAP ERP HCM to create an employee personnel number. If the candidate doesn't start as anticipated, or if you create multiple records for the same person, the data is incomplete. In these situations, when you try to delete the personnel number record, you'll get the error message: "Record cannot be deleted (time constraint 1)." If you then try to terminate the record, you'll find that the record still shows up in your turnover report. But, there's an easy fix, which you'll find in the following solution.

 Solution

The fastest way to delete a personnel number is by using Transaction PA30 or via the following menu path:

> HUMAN RESOURCES • PERSONNEL MANAGEMENT • ADMINISTRATION • HR MASTER DATA • MAINTAIN

Click the UTILITIES table at the top of your screen, choose DELETE PERSONNEL NO., and then select the employee number (PERSONNEL NO.) that you want to delete, as shown in Figure 1.

After you have selected the employee number, you will see the screen where you can select all of the infotypes and click DELETE.

After you select all of the infotypes an employee has and click on the DELETE icon, the screen shown in Figure 2 appears, asking if you really want to delete the personnel number.

18

Personnel Administration   **Part 1**

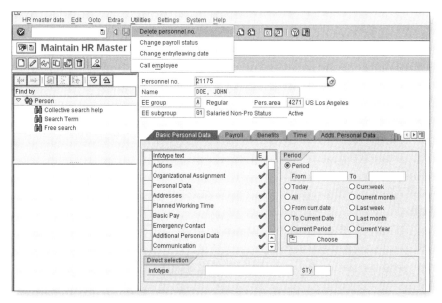

⌃ *Figure 1* PA30 Screen

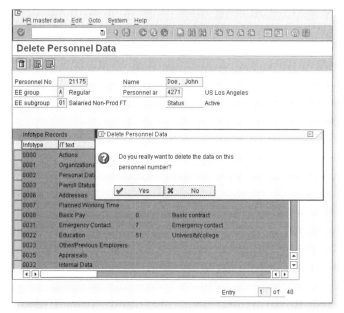

« *Figure 2*
Deleting All Infotypes

Click YES, and you'll receive a message at the bottom of your screen telling you that the personnel number was deleted completely. By being able to delete duplicate entries, you can maintain a correct employee headcount and produce accurate reporting. ■

Tip 2: Fast Entry to Maintain Master Data

You can create and edit the same infotype record for more than one employee at a time, using fast entry functionality.

If you are slowed down at work because you have to manually edit multiple employee records at a time, you can use Transaction PA70 to process multiple employee records at the same time. It's easy to create fast entries for a selected number of employees for a given infotype, saving time and effort compared to the normal processing that Transaction PA30 requires.

Solution

Transaction PA30 provides a country-specific screen for you to enter data, whereas Transaction PA70 has a single screen for all countries to enter data. The data entered via Transaction PA70 is saved in country-specific screens for the infotype. Use Transaction PA30, or go to the following menu path:

HUMAN RESOURCES • PERSONNEL MANAGEMENT • ADMINISTRATION • HR MASTER DATA • FAST ENTRY

In this example, let's create an entry for recurring payment/deductions for multiple employees using this transaction.

As shown in Figure 1, you can select the infotype that you want to create a fast entry for (in this example, we're creating an entry for a RECURRING PAYMENT/ DEDUCTIONS). For example, during the bonus increase cycle, you sometimes have to enter the bonus amount for large groups of employees into Infotype 0015 for a bonus payout. In this case, you can use Transaction PA70 and cut and paste data from a spreadsheet into this infotype. Select the infotype and click the CREATE icon.

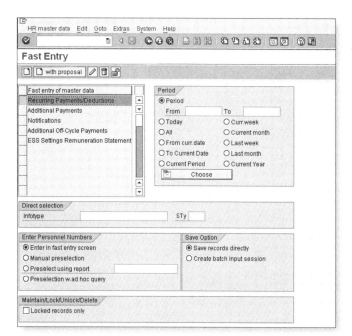

« *Figure 1*
Fast Entry Screen

Next, select the ENTER IN FAST ENTRY SCREEN button, which brings you to the screen shown in Figure 2.

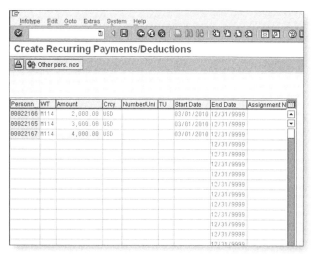

« *Figure 2*
Create Recurring Payments/Deductions

Here, you can enter the details for multiple employees manually (or by cutting and pasting them from a spreadsheet). Once you have entered the required data, click Save, which will bring you to the MAINTAIN RECURRING PAYMENT DEDUCTIONS screen, where the message records are created. ■

Tip 3 — Changing the Entry or Leaving Date

You can quickly change an employee's start or end date by using Transaction PA30.

Let's say you've hired an employee using the hiring action in SAP ERP HCM, and you realize that the start date is incorrect and needs to change. Or perhaps you've terminated an employee and the end date is incorrect. You don't want to execute another personnel action to make this change. The way to fix this is simple, as we'll see in the following solution.

Solution

In both of the scenarios described above, you can change the start/end date easily by using the standard functionality in Transaction PA30. This will change the start/end date on Infotype 0000 — Actions. Start off with the following menu path:

> HUMAN RESOURCES • PERSONNEL MANAGEMENT • ADMINISTRATION • HR MASTER DATA • MAINTAIN

Now you can select the employee record that needs to have the start or end date changed. From here, click on UTILITIES • CHANGE EMPLOYEE ENTRY/LEAVING DATE, as shown in Figure 1.

This will bring you to the CHANGE ACTIONS screen, as shown in Figure 2.

Here, you can change the START or end date in the Change (CHNG) field, depending on which one you need. Click Save, and you will receive the confirmation message "Record Changed."

Personnel Administration **Part 1**

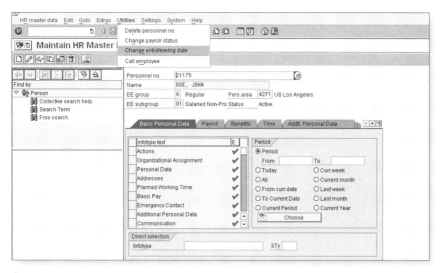

≈ *Figure 1 Change Start/End Date*

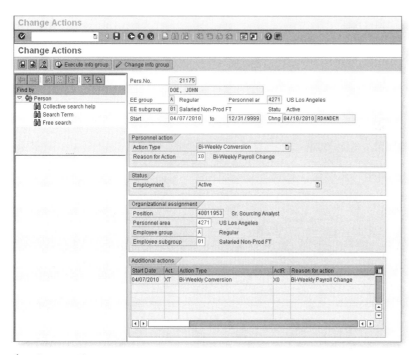

≈ *Figure 2 Change Actions*

23

Tip 4: Tracking Logged Changes in Infotype PA

Without the proper insight, it can be time-consuming trying to figure out when and how data changed in your system if you don't know where to look.

As part of the compliance data audit process (where you periodically review who logged into the system and executed which transaction on what date and whether they had authorization to do so), it's important to know which infotypes have been changed within a certain period, who changed the records, and what the change was (i.e., creation of a record, deletion of a record, etc.). The Logged Changes in Infotype RPUAUD00 — Data Report — is very useful for tracking and auditing changes to key infotypes for employee master data or applicant data. In the following solution, we'll look at how to run this report and identify any and all data that has changed in a given period.

Solution

You can see any changed data (and what those changes are) in an infotype through the add, modify, and delete functionalities using the SAP ERP HCM–delivered report RPUAUD00. While executing this program, you can list one or more infotype number that you want a report on. You can also specify a personnel number if you want see the changes that a specific employee has made. The report provides you with the details of when the data was changed, who changed the data, and which infotype it was changed in.

To execute this report, the baseline configuration setting should be completed if it isn't already done in your system.

The report can be executed for almost all infotypes (except Infotype 0008), or via the following menu path:

> HUMAN RESOURCES • PERSONNEL MANAGEMENT • ADMINISTRATION • HR MASTER DATA • INFO SYSTEM • REPORTS • DOCUMENTS • INFOTYPE CHANGES • LOGGED CHANGES IN INFOTYPE DATA

This will bring you to the LOGGED CHANGES IN INFOTYPE DATA screen, as shown in Figure 1.

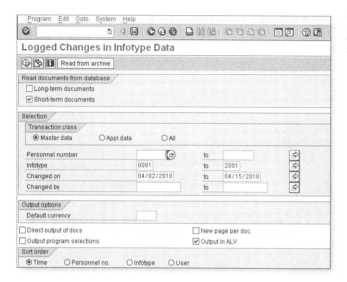

« *Figure 1*
Logged Changes in Infotype Data

Enter the INFOTYPE number(s) for which you want to create a report on logged changes. Select the master data and click Execute. This will bring you to the screen shown in Figure 2.

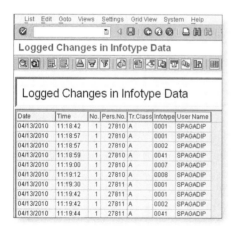

« *Figure 2*
Logged Changes in Infotype Data

Figure 2 illustrates the output of the report. As you can see, the changes that USER NAME SPAGADIP made on April 13, 2010 included a variety of infotypes. By reviewing this report monthly, you can make sure that the right people have accessed the right transactions to carry out the right tasks.

Tip 5 — Finding the Personnel Number Using Quick Search Tips

Using Quick Search, you can easily find specific personnel numbers with only a minimal amount of information.

Quick Search lets you find the personnel number of an employee — even with little information about that person. Apply the following tips to Transactions PA30, PA20, PA51, and all search help in Benefits and Time Management.

Solution

In the PERSONNEL NO. field in Transaction PA30 (Figure 1), you can use any of the criteria shown in Table 1 to find an employee.

Quick Search Code	Quick Search Code Value
Name	=n.[last name] or =n.[first name] Example : =n.Smith
Organizational assignment	=k.[personnel area] =k.[personnel subarea] =k.[employee group] =k.[employee subgroup] =k.[payroll area] =k.[company code] =k.[cost center] =k.[org unit] =k.[org key] Example: =n. PA01
Applicant	=r.[applicant number] Example: =r.smith
User ID	=u.[communication type] Example: =u.bhutoria

⌃ *Table 1 Quick Search Codes*

To search using an employee's last name, for example, you would need to write "=n.[last name]" and press Enter. The system displays the employee's personnel number. If there are multiple employee records with the same last name, it shows all of the records. To search using the first name, you would follow the same procedure: type "=n.[first name]" and press Enter.

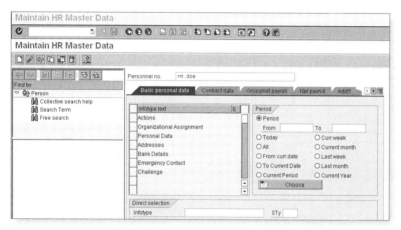

☆ *Figure 1 Personnel No. Field*

After entering the information you have (the person's last name, "=n.doe") and pressing Enter, the screen shown in Figure 2 appears.

« *Figure 2*
Quick Search Results for a Last Name Search

Figure 2 displays the employee, John Doe, using the Quick Search Tip by last name. ■

Tip 6 Creating a Personnel Administration Custom Infotype

You can easily create a personnel administration custom infotype with the field values you need by using Transaction PM01.

Often, you have to enter data in SAP ERP HCM but the standard infotypes do not have fields to store it. For example, Target Incentives and Business Key Performance Indicators are required to be stored but not delivered in standard personnel administration infotypes. Other similar business needs may require you to have a personnel administration custom infotype. You can use this custom infotype to store values in custom fields that are not available in the standard SAP infotypes. You can then create ad hoc queries and reports on this infotype.

 Solution

You can easily create a personnel administration (PA) custom infotype by using Transaction PM01 and following some simple steps. Transaction PM01 brings you to the screen shown in Figure 1.

From here, take the following steps to create your custom infotype:

1. Select the IT tab and enter the custom infotype number (INFOTYPE NO.) that you want to create. This number should be a 4-digit number and start with a 9.
2. Click the EMPLOYEE INFOTYPE button, and select the PS STRUCTURE as a SUBOBJECT.
3. Click on GENERATE OBJECTS, which brings you to a separate table maintenance window.
4. Create a PS STRUCTURE with all of the fields you want on the infotype, then save and activate the PS STRUCTURE.
5. Go back to the initial screen of Transaction PM01.

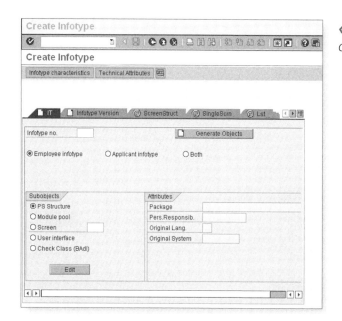

« *Figure 1*
Create Infotype

Select ALL, and then click on TECHNICAL CHARACTERISTICS, which will provide you with an infotype list screen.

1. Click on the Change (pencil) icon, and select your infotype.
2. Click on the Detail (magnifying glass) icon, and use T591A as the SUBTYPE TABLE and TS91S as the SUBTYPE TEXT tab.
3. Fill in the SUBTYPE field.
4. Save and back up to the initial Transaction PM01 screen.
5. Click on Infotype Characteristics, and once the infotype list screen appears, click on the Change icon.
6. Click on NEW ENTRIES, and enter your infotype number and short text.
7. Save your entries.

Here, we have to set different INFOTYPE CHARACTERISTICS per the requirement. At this point, it's best to open another session with some standard infotype characteristics on the screen, and use them as a reference to fill yours.

1. If you want to change the layout of the infotype, go to the initial screen of Transaction PM01, select the SCREEN radio button and list 2000 as your screen name. Click Edit.
2. Select LAYOUT EDITOR and click Change.
3. In the default layout screen, you can design or modify the screen. Change the attributes of the fields as you see fit, and be sure to Save and Activate. ■

Tip 7 — Fast Entry of Personnel Actions

Learn how you can make your data entry process faster using fast-entry actions.

Fast entry of the Personnel Actions functionality lets you enter data quickly, and even enter information into several fields in multiple infotypes using a single fast-entry screen. You can enter all of the important employee data that isn't derived from the default values, such as last name, first name, SSN, or position. Using these entries as a basis, the system fills in all of the other fields with default values.

In Customizing, you can set up your own fast-entry screens for all of the personnel action types you need by determining the content and layout of the screens for the hiring action and organizational reassignment action.

Solution

You can use Personnel Actions in SAP ERP HCM for hiring an employee, terminating an employee, and placing an employee on a leave of absence. These actions present you with required screens in the exact sequence you need for entering data. When you enter a new employee into the system, you must maintain multiple infotypes, including the employee's name, address, pay, and tax information. Fast entry for actions saves time and prevents errors in instances where you perform simple actions that don't require much data. The fast entry screen requires you to only enter data in the required fields for each infotype record. After you exit the fast entry screen, you can access the specified infotype, which enables you to add any additional data. To get to the fast entry screen, use the following menu path, which brings you to the screen in Figure 1.

> HUMAN RESOURCES • PERSONNEL MANAGEMENT • ADMINISTRATION • HR MASTER DATA • FAST ENTRY:ACTIONS

This is where you can enter the start date of the validity period for the personnel action. Choose from the list of PERSONNEL ACTIONS. In this example, let's use HIRING_NEW.

Personnel Administration **Part 1**

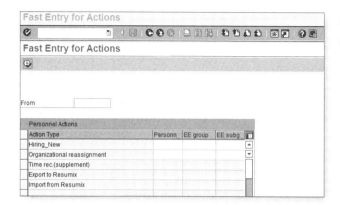

« *Figure 1*
Fast Entry for Actions

You can also enter the required information for the employee in the PERSONNEL area, employee group (EE GROUP), and employee subgroup fields. To do so, choose EXECUTE, which will bring you to the screen in Figure 2. Here, you can see the FAST DATA ENTRY FOR ACTION screen, which displays the required fields for the infotypes that define the personnel action.

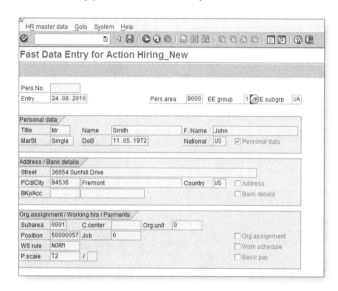

« *Figure 2*
Fast Data Entry for Action Hiring

From here, enter the appropriate data in the required fields, which is automatically stored in the infotype records.

For adding additional data into an infotype, you need to select the FURTHER INFOTYPE DATA checkbox for the corresponding infotype. After you've saved the last infotype in the infotype group, you will return to the initial screen for this infotype. Finally, be sure to save your entries.

Part 2

Organizational Management

Things You'll Learn in this Section

8	Simplifying Organizational Management Maintenance	34
9	Generating a List of Features Easily	36
10	Tracking Logged Changes to Organizational Management Data	38
11	Vacancy Tracking in Organizational Management	40
12	Maintaining Vacancy of Positions	42
13	Adding a Customer-Specific Field to a Personnel Development Infotype	44
14	Searching People and Organizational Management Objects Easily	46

In order for your company to execute numerous Human Resource–related processes, you need an organizational plan that represents the functional structure of your enterprise based on the tasks it needs to complete. Organizational Management (OM) provides a basis for the organizational plan, HR components, and the business workflow that creates the framework for a routing structure to assign tasks to an employee for completion. This section of tips will help developers, business analysts, system administrators, and functional power-users in HR and IT with OM data administration in SAP ERP HCM. Topics covered include OM objects, relationships, infotypes, data audits, searches, and reports.

Tip 8: Simplifying Organizational Management Maintenance

Organizational Management relationships and infotypes can be confusing and difficult to remember. Making changes to Organizational Management objects, such as structure, units, jobs, and positions is much easier using Transaction PPOME.

All organizations evolve and change over time. For example, you may need to change a position, organizational unit, or job description. Making changes to Organizational Management objects is easier using Transaction PPOME. This method has an advantage over the expert mode of maintenance — you don't have to be familiar with object types, relationships codes, and evaluation paths. Transaction PPOME provides you with a visual interface to select the object you want to change. Performing recurring maintenance is easier and less time-consuming when searching with the Object Manager.

 Solution

You can simplify the maintenance of Organizational Management objects, such as the organizational unit, jobs, and positions by using Transaction PPOME to:

- Change the text of an organizational unit or position
- Change the account assignment of the personnel area, personnel subarea, employee group, and employee subgroup to a position
- Change the basic data and related relationships using this functionality

You can use Transaction PPOME, or go to the following menu path:

> HUMAN RESOURCES • ORGANIZATIONAL MANAGEMENT • ORGANIZATIONAL PLAN • ORGANIZATION AND STAFFING • CHANGE

As you can see in Figure 1, you can select any object, such as POSITION or ORGANIZATIONAL UNIT, that you want to change.

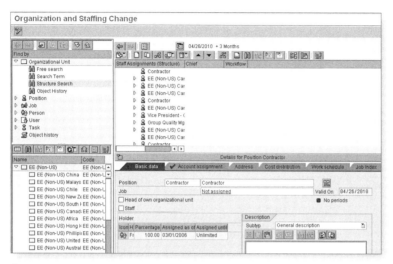

▲ Figure 1 Organization and Staffing Change

As you can see, you can select and highlight the object that you want to change. For example, to rename a position, simply highlight the position by clicking on it and in the section below DETAILS FOR POSITION CONTRACTOR, you make changes to the POSITION name text and click Save. You'll see the changes reflected in Figure 2.

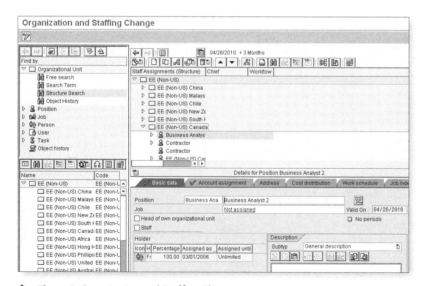

▲ Figure 2 Organization and Staffing Change

Tip 9: Generating a List of Features Easily

It's easy to generate a list of all of the features used in SAP ERP HCM according to your specific search criteria.

Features are frequently used to determine default values. These values are proposed by the system when employee master data infotypes are maintained. Feature ABKRS, for example, provides a default value for the payroll group. This is based upon the information found in an employee's Organizational Assignment infotype. Feature LGMST also illustrates this concept — it proposes permissible wage types for an employee in the Basic Payments infotype, based on personnel and pay-scale structures.

There are a large number of features in the SAP ERP HCM system, and it can be very difficult even for frequent users to remember all the names and how to access them. In this tip, you will learn how to easily access a list of all features using a simple report RPUMKD00 for future reference and use.

 Solution

You can search for a particular feature in a variety of ways. The search criteria for the features list includes:

- Name of the feature
- Persons responsible for the feature
- Feature type
- Feature version
- Activation indicator for the feature

The first results list for the report provides you with the following information for each entry:

- Name, type, and version of the feature
- ABAP Dictionary structure
- Persons responsible for the feature
- Status for each entry

To generate a list of the features you need, execute the report RPUMKD00 by going to Transaction SE38 and clicking on SELECT REPORT RPUMKD00, which displays the list of features.

In the results list, you can display the respective attributes and documentation for each of these features. In addition, you can access the INITIAL SCREEN for the feature you have selected. To do this, choose EDIT. You can then display or change the individual elements for the feature.

Click Execute for the report as shown in Figure 1. You can also search for a specific feature using the search criteria as specified previously.

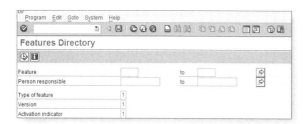

« *Figure 1*
Features Directory

In Figure 1, you can enter the name of the feature or leave it blank to get a complete list of features. Once you click Execute, you'll see the screen shown in Figure 2.

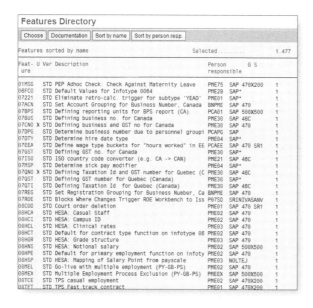

« *Figure 2*
Features Directory

This displays the list of all features with a short DESCRIPTION. You can choose FEATURE from this screen and click to maintain it.

Tip 10 Tracking Logged Changes to Organizational Management Data

You can easily audit changes made to OM data using the standard delivered report RHRHAZ00. You can do a recurring/regular review of your OM data changes using this report and also save snapshots of your audit report.

As a frequent user of the Organizational Management (OM) function in SAP ERP HCM, you want to monitor or track changes that have been made to OM objects such as Jobs, Positions, and Organizational units. You could easily and effectively track the changes to OM objects. You can find out who created OM objects and when they were created. And you can monitor the most recent changes to objects based on dates in your selection criteria. You can also verify the data for accuracy and check if it follows your company approval process.

The SAP standard delivered report RHRHAZ00 lets you track changes to your OM data and you can also use report RHRHAZ00 to take periodic snapshots of your OM data and save it in Excel or another file format, and file it for compliance purposes or further analyses. The report provides you with changes to OM objects. This enables you to track changes to OM objects and complete your audit process. Also, you can validate changes for accuracy and maintain your data integrity.

✓ Solution

To track changes to OM objects such as organizational units, jobs, and positions, you need to execute report RHRHAZ00. This report will give you an output with results displaying the object ID that was changed. The infotype number that was changed for the object ID, subtype of the infotype, start and end date of the infotype, date changed on and the user ID of the person who made the changes. To execute report RHRHAZ0000, enter Transaction SE38, then enter RHRHAZ00 in the PROGRAM field.

Click the Execute icon. You will see the selection screen of the report as shown in Figure 1.

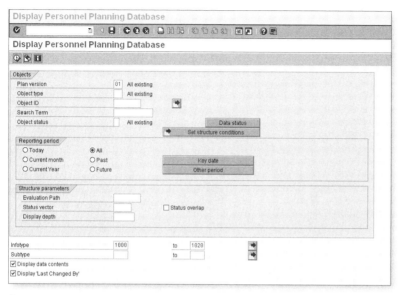

⚠ *Figure 1* Display Personnel Planning Database

Enter the INFOTYPE NUMBER and the OBJECT ID in the selection screen you want to audit or track changes, and click on the Execute icon. You will then see the report output as shown in Figure 2.

⚠ *Figure 2* Display Personnel Planning Database — Report Output

Tip 11: Vacancy Tracking in Organizational Management

You can use the standard SAP ERP HCM report RHXFILLPOS to display, modify, and use open or vacant positions as needed.

Keeping track of open or vacant positions can be very challenging if you are not using Vacancy Tracking in the Organizational Management functionality in SAP ERP HCM. Often, the unused or nondelimited positions appear in headcount reports, other OM reports, or manager views in self-service applications. Identifying and fixing inaccurate data quickly and efficiently allows resources to be spent in more productive activities.

In this tip, you'll learn how to execute the HR report RHXFILLPOS. This report lets you track all of the unoccupied positions without using Infotype 1007 — Vacancy Tracking. This will let you keep track of unoccupied positions and clean-up unused or unoccupied positions, ultimately resulting in more accurate reporting.

Solution

Using report RHXFILLPOS or the following menu path, you can list all of the open positions for a given time period across all organizational units. This report provides the start and end dates, the total number of days open, and the titles of positions.

> HUMAN RESOURCES • ORGANIZATIONAL MANAGEMENT • INFO SYSTEM • POSITION • PERIOD WHEN POSITIONS ARE UNOCCUPIED

Choose the report and you will see the selection screen shown in Figure 1.

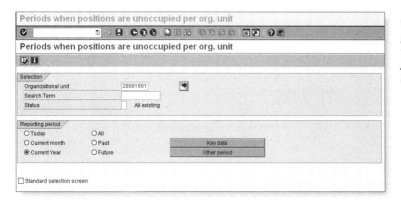

« **Figure 1**
Displays Period When Positions Are Vacant / Unoccupied

In the selection screen, you can choose the ORGANIZATIONAL UNIT for which you want to determine the positions that are unoccupied or have remained unoccupied for a given period of time and click Execute. You will see the report output, as shown in Figure 2.

« **Figure 2**
Periods When Positions Are Unoccupied per Org Unit Report Output

The report displays the output by ORGANIZATIONAL UNIT, and the POSITION and the unoccupied periods (UNOCC. FROM and UNOCC. TO). It also shows the total number of days the position has remained unoccupied. You can track positions with your recruiting and HR teams to check on the steps being taken to fill them (UNOCC. DAYS). ∎

Tip 12 — Maintaining Vacancy of Positions

You can track and maintain vacant positions using Infotype 1007, which lets you report on vacant positions and can integrate with your recruiting system.

Vacancy Tracking lets you effectively manage your positions and headcount reporting. You can designate your positions as open (vacant) or filled using Infotype 1007. To use this functionality you'll need to enable vacancy processing during customization. When a new position is created, it is marked as open. Once you hire, transfer, or promote an employee to fill this position, it is marked as "vacancy filled." For example, when you hire someone and place them into a position, you will see a dialog box that asks if you wish to delimit the vacancy. Selecting Yes, as position is no longer vacant, changes Infotype 1007 to vacancy filled.

Similarly, when you terminate someone using the termination action, a dialog box will appear asking if you wish to create a vacancy. Clicking the Yes button changes Infotype 1007 to open. Clicking No will leave Infotype 1007 with a value of vacancy filled, though there is no one holding the position.

 ## Solution

You can maintain a position as vacant or filled using Infotype 1007, which is maintained on a position. To access this infotype, you can use Transaction PP01 or go to the following menu path:

> HUMAN RESOURCES • ORGANIZATIONAL MANAGEMENT • EXPERT MODE POSITION

As shown in Figure 1, you can choose the POSITION you want to mark as vacant and select the VACANCY infotype.

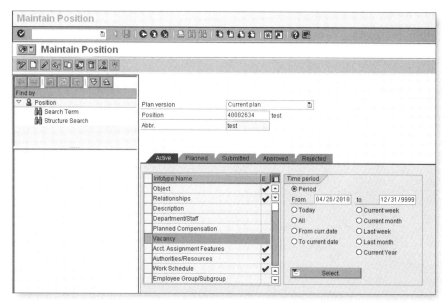

⌃ Figure 1 Maintain Position

Once you click on the SELECT button, you'll see the screen shown in Figure 2, where you can add a vacancy to a position.

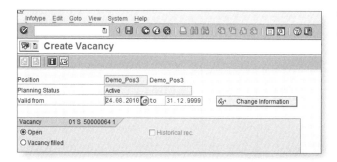

« Figure 2
Add Vacancy

As you can see from Figure 2, you can mark a position as OPEN (vacant) or VACANCY FILLED. The record is date-driven, so a position, for example, can be vacant for 3 months and occupied for 1 year, and vacant again for 2 months. The history is maintained in Infotype 1007.

To tract vacant positions and their history, use the vacant positions report RHVOPOSO. You can also integrate this infotype with your recruiting system and share vacant positions data. ∎

Tip 13 — Adding a Customer-Specific Field to a Personnel Development Infotype

You can easily add a custom field to an existing Personnel Development infotype to store data in a field not delivered with standard the SAP system.

Often, there is a need to add a custom field in Personnel Development infotypes. For example, you need to update Infotype 1003 — Departments/Staff — as part of your maintenance for organizational units. There is a requirement to add a new custom field, called Projects, to show the number of budgeted positions the organizational unit had at the beginning of the year.

✓ Solution

These types of enhancements can be implemented rather easily, however, it's important to note that you can only enhance infotypes that can be maintained directly. You can determine whether an infotype can be maintained directly when customizing for Organizational Management (OM) you are in the MAINTAIN INFOTYPES activity and are in the INFOTYPES PER OBJECT view. Another way of displaying all of the relevant infotypes is to display all of the entries from the Infotypes per Object Type table (T777I) for which the MAINT field (cannot be maintained using standard transactions) has been activated. It's important to remember that the standard infotypes, Infotypes 1000 (Object) and 1001 (Relationships) are excluded from any enhancements.

To add a custom field, start the Personnel Planning infotype copier (Transaction PPCI) or use the following menu path (shown in Figure 1):

> HUMAN RESOURCES • PERSONNEL MANAGEMENT • ORG MANAGEMENT • DETAIL MAINTENANCE

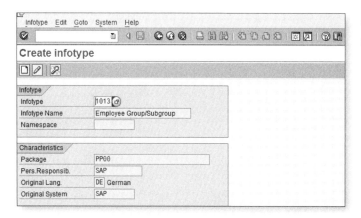

« *Figure 1*
Create Infotype

In the INFOTYPE field, enter the four-digit number of the infotype you want to enhance and choose EXTEND. Next, you can specify an enhancement category using EXTRAS. Define the customer-specific components (infotype fields) in the ENHANCEMENT CATEGORY. Now, check the structure and activate it.

You have now added the fields created in the structure CI_Pnnnn to the infotype you selected. The following objects were created in the process:

▶ CI_Include CI_Pnnnn

▶ An include-specific module pool ZPnnnn00

▶ An include screen ZPnnnn000200

To enhance the list screen, go to INFOTYPE • ENHANCE LIST SCREEN • SUBOBJECTS • ADDITIONAL LIST FIELDS.

1. First, create the structure ZPLISnnnn, so choose GENERATE OBJECTS.

2. Specify an enhancement category using EXTRAS • ENHANCEMENT CATEGORY and define the customer-specific components (infotype fields).

3. Fill the customer-specific fields in the list structure by adding ZPLISnnnn-Customerfield1 = Pnnnn-Customerfield1 to each field.

4. Activate the INCLUDE AFTER THE SYNTAX HAS BEEN CONFIRMED. Check the structure and activate it.

You have just added a custom field to Infotype PD. ■

Tip 14 — Searching People and Organizational Management Objects Easily

SAP ERP HCM includes a tool called the Object Manager, which contains features that help you to reduce the number of steps required to complete searches easily.

Often, searching for an employee in Organizational Management (OM) is sometimes difficult and it is more confusing when you are searching multiple employees. You can make your life easier by using Object Manager. The Object Manager is a search tool within SAP ERP HCM. This tool is similar to Field Search Help. In Field Search Help, you can select records, employees, or objects from a dropdown list and then you go back again to select the next record. The Object Manager makes it easier for you by saving the search hit list and displaying it on the screen. You can easily select an object or record and process it, then select the next one from the hit list without having to perform the search again.

In this tip, you'll learn how to use the Object Manager to eliminate two steps for every subsequent employee. You won't need to search repeatedly — you can reuse employees from the hit list. Using the Object Manager, you can search for employees in multiple ways, including by search term, structure search, and free search. You will benefit from the Object Manager when you have to perform a similar task on a group of employees.

 Solution

The Object Manager Search functionality is a transaction code–based search. In the following example, you can search Organizational Management Objects, such as organizational units, jobs, and positions using Transaction PPOME, or by using the following menu path:

> HUMAN RESOURCES • ORGANIZATIONAL MANAGEMENT • ORGANIZATIONAL PLAN • ORGANIZATION AND STAFFING • CHANGE

Figure 1 shows the Object Manager as it appears in Transaction PPOME.

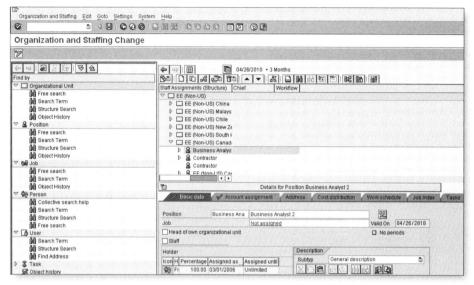

↥ Figure 1 Organizational and Staffing Change

You can search using SEARCH TERM help. This tool lets you search for anyone who reports directly or indirectly to a specified organizational unit or position. Figure 2 shows the SEARCH TERM window prepared to locate all of the employees who belong to ORGANIZATIONAL UNIT EE (NON U.S.). Once the OBJECT displays the list of the EMPLOYEES, you can use the list to complete processing your maintenance work.

« Figure 2
Organizational and Staffing
Change Search Term

Part 3
Benefits

Things You'll Learn in this Section

15	Changing Employee Benefits Using Adjustment Reasons	50
16	Hide-Optional Fields on Benefits Infotypes	52
17	Using the Benefits Toolset Plan Cost Summary Report	54
18	Creating a New Benefit Plan Faster by Copying an Existing Plan	56
19	Overriding the Benefit Salary on Life Insurance	58
20	Controlling Open Enrollment with an Adjustment Reason	60
21	Managing Year-End Adjustment Payroll Runs for Terminated Employees	62

Benefits are a critical component of the total compensation employers offer to attract and retain employees. Streamlined benefit administration activities, combined with direct access to structured benefits data to assist in decision making, will help your organization to contain or even cut costs. Employee Self-Service (ESS), for example, can significantly reduce paperwork, questions, or issues processed by your benefits staff, and at the same time improve data accuracy. Employee satisfaction increases with up-to-the-minute information about benefits elections, and access to information to support decision-making. This section of tips will help developers, business analysts, system administrators, and functional power-users in HR and IT with benefits processing and data administration in SAP ERP HCM.

Tip 15 Changing Employee Benefits Using Adjustment Reasons

You can control changes to employee benefits enrollments using well-defined benefit adjustment reasons.

Employees cannot elect to add, change, or cancel coverage at any time during a plan year unless there is a "qualifying event" (e.g., marriage, leave of absence, divorce, birth of a child, etc.). To accommodate such exceptions, an adjustment reason is created for employees to let them add, change, or stop participation in a benefit plan. Adjustment reasons can be defined within Configuration, and are assigned as subtypes in Infotype 0378 — Adjustment Reasons Records — in the HR master data. This infotype can only have one record at a time. The Adjustment Reasons Record allows an employee to make changes to their benefits enrollment.

A Benefit Adjustment Reason also controls changes permitted to each Benefit Plan type (e.g., medical, insurance, or flexible spending account). In this tip, you'll learn how to add new Benefit Adjustment Reasons for qualifying events. Using well-defined adjustment reasons provides you with better control over benefits enrollment for your employees. So, let's get started.

 Solution

You can easily create a new adjustment reason for qualifying events. You can also manage exceptions by adding special adjustment reasons. To do this, navigate to the IMG via the following menu path:

> PERSONNEL MANAGEMENT • BENEFITS • FLEXIBLE ADMINISTRATION • BENEFITS ADJUSTMENT REASONS • DEFINE BENEFIT ADJUSTMENT REASONS.

This is where you can define the new adjustment reasons. Once you have created a new adjustment reason, you can define the permissions for each plan type or any adjustment groupings you may have defined. To do so, take the following steps:

- Click on BENEFIT ADJUSTMENT REASONS, and choose NEW ENTRIES.
- Enter a four-character identifier and description for your new adjustment reason.
- Define the time frame for changes to enrollments.
  - In the TOTAL TIME ALLOWED FOR ADJUSTMENTS field, you can enter the timeframe within which changes must be made. In the TIME ALLOWED FOR ADJUSTMENTS AFTER INITIAL CHOICE field, you can enter a shorter time period during which changes are allowed after an employee has made their initial selection.
  - Select CHANGES ANYTIME if you want to allow changes to enrollments at any time, regardless of whether or not an employee has an Adjustment Reason Record (Infotype 0378) for the adjustment reason in question. If you define an adjustment reason as ANYTIME, you don't need to define time restrictions.
- Enter the validity dates for the benefit plan records created by adjustment processing.
- Save your entries and you'll be brought to the screen shown in Figure 1.

« Figure 1
New Entries — Details of Added Entries

Tip 16: Hide-Optional Fields on Benefits Infotypes

In SAP ERP, you can easily hide fields or tabs in the benefits infotypes that may not be relevant to your company's business requirements.

You can simplify the end users' benefits entry screen by hiding fields that are not required (optional). To do so, you'll need to revise table T588M and create a module pool within the table for each different screen within an infotype. Note: Each tab is assigned to a screen number. In this tip, you'll learn how to simplify your benefits entry screens by hiding fields that aren't necessary for your business needs.

 Solution

In this example, we'll use the Benefits Infotype. To hide fields on a Benefit infotype, you'll need to select the infotype in table T588M. You can click the radio button under the HIDE column for each field you want to hide. Note: There are a few exceptions. You cannot hide the DEPENDANTS tab on Infotype 0167, or the Beneficiaries tab on Infotab 0168.

Be sure to Save your entries. This will trigger a transport request. Be sure to save changes in a Transport request so that after testing you can transport your changes to your production system.

To get to table T588M, use the following menu path:

> PERSONNEL MANAGEMENT • PERSONNEL ADMINISTRATION • CUSTOMIZING USER INTERFACES • CHANGE SCREEN MODIFICATION

Click on SCREEN MODIFICATIONS, and select the BENEFIT INFOTYPE for which you want to hide fields. In this example, shown in Figure 1, we'll use Infotype 0167 — Health Plan — to hide a few fields.

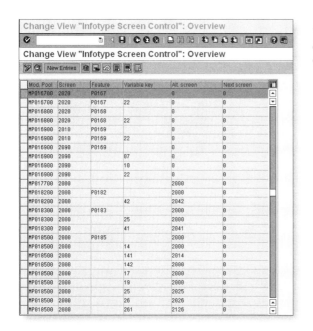

« Figure 1
Change View Infotype Screen Control — Overview

From here, you can select the Infotype 0167 Health Plan, and click on the Details icon (magnifying glass). This will bring you to the screen shown in Figure 2.

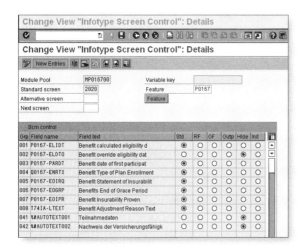

« Figure 2
Change View Infotype Screen Control — Details

In this screen, select the fields you want to hide by selecting the radio button under the HIDE column, and be sure to Save. Use Transaction PA30 to open Infotype 0167 for a sample employee, and you will find that the fields that you chose are now hidden on Infotype 0167's record.

Tip 17: Using the Benefits Toolset Plan Cost Summary Report

The cost, options, and details for your health insurance are at your fingertips with a benefits toolset Plan Cost summary report.

Employee benefits are an important part of running a business in today's market. They can provide a competitive advantage in attracting and retaining talent. Many companies spend a significant amount of resources on benefits for their employees. Costs continue to increase, and management needs easy-access information about the various benefit, insurance, and miscellaneous plans configured in their systems. Access to the options, coverage, and costs of employee, employer, and provider plans is crucial to making intelligent business decisions regarding annual plan changes.

The Plan Cost Summary report lets you access all of this information. It's easy to execute and provides a quick overview of all of the benefit plan's costs and details as they have been set up in your system. Using this report, your benefits planning and decision making will be much easier and more productive.

Solution

In the Plan Cost Summary report, the details of your benefit plan information are broken down into the following:

- Cost details for health plan by plan and plan option
- Cost details for insurance plans by plan and coverage
- Cost details for miscellaneous plans by plan and plan options

This report is executed using the standard SAP-delivered Benefit toolset. You can execute this report based on the Benefit Area, Plan Type, and Benefit Plan. In addition, you can also select multiple plans. If you leave the PLAN TYPE field blank, the system selects all plans in the PLAN TYPE. For example, if you select the Plan TYPE MEDI (Medical) and leave PLAN blank, the report will provide output for all medical plans. To get to the PLAN COST SUMMARY, use the following menu path:

PERSONNEL MANAGEMENT • BENEFITS • TOOLSET • PLAN COST SUMMARY.

Select the PLAN COST SUMMARY and click on the green checkmark, which brings you to the screen shown in Figure 1.

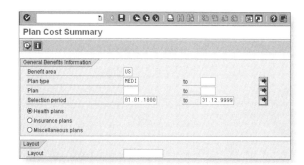

« *Figure 1*
Plan Cost Summary Report

Enter the BENEFIT AREA using the drop-down menu. In this example, we have chosen US. Enter the PLAN TYPE for which you want to report, and leave the PLAN field blank if you want to report on all plans. After you execute the report you will see the results screen, as shown in Figure 2. This report displays an overview of all your plans.

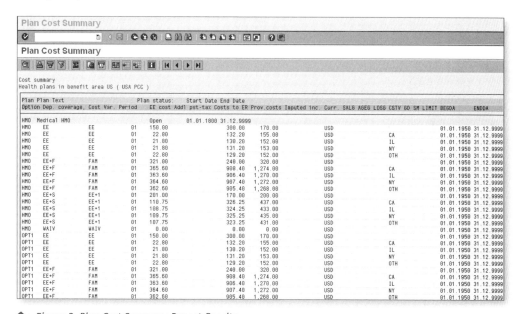

⌃ *Figure 2* *Plan Cost Summary Report Results*

Tip 18 — Creating a New Benefit Plan Faster by Copying an Existing Plan

You can quickly and easily configure a new benefit plan in your SAP ERP HCM system using the Copy Benefit Plan functionality.

Employee benefit plans need to be flexible. Business conditions are dynamic and employee's needs may change over time. It's not uncommon for a company to add a new plan to their benefit offerings. Adding a new plan can often be a tedious and time-consuming process because it requires the Information Technology department to configure all of the changes in the system.

However, you can easily add the new plan by using the Copy Benefit Plan functionality, which is useful if a particular benefit plan already exists with similar attributes to the benefit plan that needs to be created. You can copy the existing plan and modify as necessary, rather than building a plan from scratch. Basically, you select a plan to copy, enter the new plan description, and make your changes. Let's dive into the specific steps in the following text.

✓ Solution

To create a new plan, it is often best to copy an existing plan and make changes to suit your needs. For example, there is an existing plan in your health plan offering. You want to create a new plan that is similar, but with different costs.

The only limitation of this functionality is that you cannot copy a plan into a different benefit area than the benefit area of the original plan. To start you need to select the existing plan to copy and enter the new plan's description. This allows you to copy all of the customizing entries for a benefit plan within a benefit area and duplicate them under a new plan name.

> PERSONNEL MANAGEMENT • BENEFITS • TOOLSET • COPY BENEFIT PLAN

1. Click on Copy Benefit Plan and enter the Benefit area from the drop-down menu for your country.
2. Select the source Benefit Plan that you want to copy, and enter the New Benefit Plan four-digit identifier code. Fill in the Name of new benefit plan field, as illustrated in Figure 1.

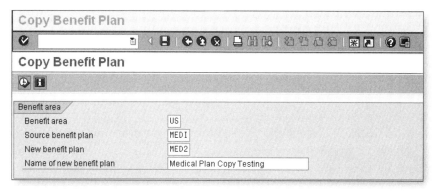

˄ *Figure 1* Copy Benefit Plan

Click Execute. You will receive a confirmation message asking you if you want your newly created benefit plan to be successfully copied to the old benefit plan.

3. Select Yes, and then the system will ask you if the changes should be transported.
4. Select Yes again, and then Save the changes in a transport.

Once you have done this, you have officially created a new health plan. You can now go to cost rules and change the cost values for this new plan.

Tip 19 — Overriding the Benefit Salary on Life Insurance

You can override a salary to correct the amount of insurance coverage for group.

Often, Infotype 0008 for a current year is not a true representation of an employee's salary for life insurance calculations in Infotype 0168. For example, if your company has recently implemented salary reductions but has granted exceptions to allow life insurance coverage to be the same limit as before the salary changes, then you need to override the current benefit salary in Infotype 0168. Another example would be granting an executive higher coverage as an exception.

In this tip, you'll learn how to enter a new benefit salary in the salary override field and change the basic insurance coverage to display the new correct coverage amount. No ABAP is required to achieve this change. This process will save you time and effort in managing the accuracy of your insurance plan coverage. So, let's get started.

 Solution

You can adjust the life insurance coverage amount via Transaction PA30, Infotype 0168, and entering the salary in the SALARY OVERRIDE field. By doing this, a new Infotype 0168 record with salary override gets created.

To make the salary override reflect the correct insurance coverage amount:

1. Enter the new benefit salary in the SALARY OVERRIDE field in Infotype 0168 under the INSURANCE COVERAGE tab.
2. Enter the effective dates for the new record and press `Enter`.
3. Click Save. A new Infotype 0168 record when the salary override is created. THE NEW BASIC COVERAGE amount will be displayed under the INSURANCE COVERAGE field. This override salary will be used to calculate the new insurance coverage amount, as shown in Figure 1, which you can get to via the following menu path:

HUMAN RESOURCES • PERSONNEL MANAGEMENT • ADMINISTRATION • HR MASTER DATA

Select an employee record and Infotype 0168.

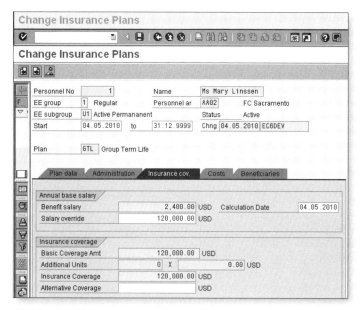

↥ *Figure 1* Change Insurance Plan

In Infotype 0168, select the Insurance Coverage (INSURANCE COV.) tab and enter the salary override amount on the SALARY OVERRIDE field. You will see the new insurance coverage amount in the INSURANCE COVERAGE field when you execute standard reports on benefits you will see the new coverage amount. ■

Tip 20 Controlling Open Enrollment with an Adjustment Reason

You can manage open enrollment differently by allowing certain employees to make changes to certain benefit elections.

The standard delivered Open Enrollment (OE) in SAP ERP HCM process allows all employees to change their benefit selections. Some companies may desire to manage this process differently. For example, companies with large populations could divide the employees into groups and offer each a different enrollment period. This will help your benefits team manage the OE process, and reduce Employee Self-Services (ESS) performance challenges by having smaller groups accessing the system at a given time.

You can implement this type of control by configuring an adjustment reason and assigning it to an employee record in Infotype 0378. You can also control the validity of the OE period by the validity period of the Adjustment Reason. You need to make sure a General Benefits Information (Infotype 0171) record exists before you create an Adjustment Reasons (Infotype 0378) record for an employee for Adjustment Reason Open Enrollment.

 Solution

To allow certain employees to process OE, you can configure an Adjustment Reason called "Open Enrollment." Assign the adjustment reason to an employee record in Infotype 0378. Changes that are possible using this adjustment reason are controlled per plan type by adjustment permissions. These permissions are assigned to a combination of adjustment reasons and employee groups in Customizing.

Configuring and customizing an adjustment reason is easy. Under your IMG settings, turn off your Standard OE process by selecting OPEN ENROLLMENT NOT ALLOWED, by going to:

> PERSONNEL MANAGEMENT • BENEFITS • FLEXIBLE ADMINISTRATION • BENEFITS ADJUSTMENT REASONS • DEFINE BENEFIT ADJUSTMENT REASONS

After you click on BENEFIT ADJUSTMENT REASONS, you can take the following steps:

1. Choose New entries.
2. Enter a four-character identifier and description for your new adjustment reason.
3. Define the time frame for changes to enrollments.
   - In the TOTAL TIME ALLOWED FOR ADJUSTMENTS field, you can enter the time within which changes must be made for open enrollment.
   - In the TIME ALLOWED FOR ADJUST field, you can then enter a shorter time period during which changes to the employees initial choices are allowed.
4. Enter validity dates for benefit plan records created by the OE.
5. Save your entries, which will bring you to the screen shown in Figure 1.

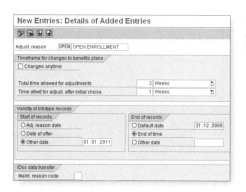

« *Figure 1 Benefit Adjustment Reason Screen*

Next, you need to configure the changes allowed for each plan type. The company allows employees to change plans, options, and dependents, and even discontinue participation in a plan during OE. So, Figure 2 shows the adjustment permissions for a medical insurance plan.

« *Figure 2 New Entries — Details of Added Entries*

You have now configured an Adjustment Reason (ADJUST. REASON) for OE. You can assign this ADJUST. REASON to employees by creating an Infotype 0378 record. The existence of this record will allow employees to do OE via the Adjustment Reason in ESS and through the standard OE screens in the SAP system. ■

Tip 21 — Managing Year-End Adjustment Payroll Runs for Terminated Employees

You can use Infotype 0221 to carry out year-end adjustment payroll run dates for your terminated employees.

There are often problems related to processing terminated employees. For example, if you are processing year-end adjustments using the workbench with Infotype 0221 and you want a check date of 12/31/XXXX. When you execute the adjustment run with payroll run type B and an adjustment special run date of 01/15/YYYY, it could result in an error message stating the employee is inactive and processing will stop.

Another problem often arises when terminated employees are related to Payroll area changes. A year-end adjustment payroll run can fail to process an Infotype 0221 record (subtype YANA) for a terminated employee. For example, the employee in question was terminated in period 21 and a termination payroll run was performed. The same employee was reinstated in a different payroll area for the whole of pay period 26 (from November 28 to December 11) with a direct deposit date of December 30. Payroll results for pay period 26 were created. A subtype YANA record was entered with a date of November 27. An adjustment payroll run (run type B) was performed using the special run date 02/18/YYYY in the original payroll area. This action failed to process the employee. Pay period 4 of YYYY (with a deposit date of 02/17/YYYY) is now closed. Even specifying the correct Infotype 0221 pay date for the terminated employee (either the termination date or the pay date of the last payroll result) failed to resolve the problem.

 Solution

You can easily avoid these kinds of problems if you carry out year-end adjustment payroll runs for terminated employees by managing Infotype 0221. For example, when entering dates on Infotype 0221 for terminated employees in the foreground (i.e., online), you must change the check date of 12/31/XXXX to the pay date of the employee's most recent payroll result. If you are entering the dates for terminated employees on Infotype 0221 in the background (i.e., batch input), the system automatically changes this date, provided that the adjustment processed for the terminated employee is in the prior year.

Problems arising from terminated employees related to Payroll area changes can be addressed via a Payroll Area Change solution. The date of the adjustment on Infotype 0221 must equal either the termination date or the end date of the most recent payroll result for the employee. For BDC input, it's simpler to use the employee's termination date.

Because the payroll area changes solution occurred and payroll results were created for subsequent periods, the adjustment payroll run must be started within the new payroll area rather than the payroll area to which the adjustment belongs. But, the adjustment process ensures that the original payroll area will be adjusted. As a rule, when performing special runs, make sure to use the payroll area actually assigned to the employee on the selected pay or special run date.

To maintain Infotype 0221, you can use Transaction PA30 or go to:

> HUMAN RESOURCES • PERSONNEL MANAGEMENT • ADMINISTRATION • MAINTAIN MASTER DATA • MAINTAIN

Select Infotype 0221 and the employee record you want to process and update the dates in the foreground to maintain the records, as shown in Figure 1.

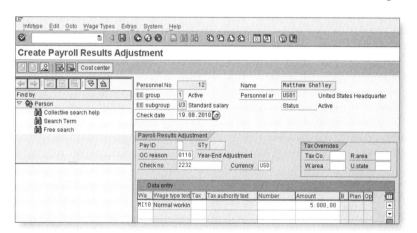

⌃ *Figure 1* Create Payroll Results Adjustment

Part 4

Payroll

Things You'll Learn in this Section

22	Deleting Old Payroll Processes	66
23	Changing the Earliest Retro-Accounting Date/Master Data Change on Payroll Status	68
24	Reversing Your Posting Run Documents	70
25	Auditing Payroll and Time Schema with Subschemas and PCRs	72
26	Displaying Deleted Payroll Results	74
27	Inserting Custom Messages in Employee Pay Stubs	76
28	Performing Special and Year-End Adjustments for Payroll	80
29	Updating Payroll Schemas and PCRs with Line Editor Commands	82
30	Creating Files for Third Party Providers	84
31	Deleting Current Payroll Results for an Employee	88

Paying employees is a primary function within any organization. At a minimum it's a combination of complicated calculations to determine the remuneration, tax amounts, insurance amounts, and other pay of an employee for a particular period of time. It uses data from personnel administration and benefits under a wide variety of configurations. This section of tips will help developers, business analysts, system administrators, and functional power-users in HR and IT who are interested in completing payroll administration in SAP ERP HCM in a more efficient and effective manner.

Tip 22 Deleting Old Payroll Processes

Deleting your old payroll processes will significantly improve your payroll process workbench performance.

Every time you execute a payroll process during your regular or off-cycle payroll run, it automatically creates and runs a series of programs. Each regular or off-cycle payroll process that runs is saved. These saved processes, if not deleted, create an extensive backlog of old processes that quickly and negatively impact system performance.

You can routinely delete the old saved processes using the standard delivered program H99UCDP0 in SAP ERP HCM.

 Solution

Before you permanently delete any saved payroll processes, you should first determine which processes are obsolete and ready for deletion. To do this, use program H99UCDP0 by going to Transaction SE38 and clicking on ENTER REPORT NAME. First, execute the report in simulation mode by checking the TEST checkbox. They are displayed and you can carefully review the report output. When satisfied with the results in simulation, you can run the report by deselecting the checkbox.

- In the selection screen, select the OBSOLETE PROCESSES checkbox, based on processes status.
- Indicate the CREATION DATE range to select the process identified in the previous step.
- Test the report in the simulation by checking the TEST checkbox and executing the report. When satisfied with the results, you can then execute the actual report by deselecting the TEST checkbox and running the report. The automatic completion and deletion of processes results are displayed in the screen shown in Figure 1.

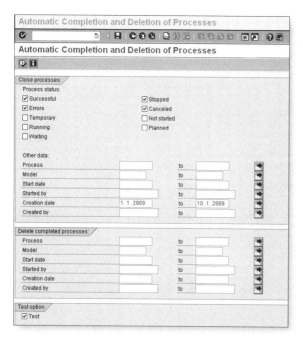

« *Figure 1*
Automatic Completion and Deletion Processes

In this screen, you can check the boxes in the PROCESS STATUS that you want deleted. In this example, we selected SUCCESSFUL, STOPPED, ERRORS, and CANCELED. Next, enter the CREATION DATE or date range for the process to be selected for deletion. Select the TEST checkbox, and click Execute. The results will be the processes selected for deletion. Once you've reviewed the results, deselect the TEXT checkbox, and click Execute.

Your old payroll processes have now been permanently deleted, as you can see in Figure 2.

« *Figure 2*
Automatic Completion and Deletion of Process

Tip 23: Changing the Earliest Retro-Accounting Date/Master Data Change on Payroll Status

You can manually set the retroactive accounting limit for an employee with Infotype 0003 — Payroll Status.

Infotype 0003 — Payroll Status — is created automatically by the system during a hiring action and is automatically maintained for each payroll period.

There are situations when you'll need to change the earliest retroactive accounting date or earliest master data change for a particular payroll run. When payroll is processed, the system does a retroactive calculation and picks up records of one-time changes, which will change the earliest master data change date. To prevent this, you can manually change the earliest master data change and earliest retroactive accounting date to the current date or a date you specify. The system will not pick up records older than the date specified. Payroll can use this process to stop the system from triggering any retroactive accounting. The system would only process those changes up to the specified earliest retroactive accounting date. So, let's get started.

Solution

To change the earliest retroactive accounting date of an employee record in Infotype 0003, select the employee via Transaction PA30 and then select UTILITIES • CHANGE PAYROLL STATUS. This brings up the Infotype 0003 record. Here, you can change the earliest master data change or earliest retroactive accounting Date for an employee.

You can implement mass changes to Infotype 0003 for multiple employees by using Report RPUCRR00, or via the following menu path:

> HUMAN RESOURCES • PERSONNEL MANAGEMENT • ADMINISTRATION • HR MASTER DATA

As shown in Figure 1, click on UTILITIES, and select CHANGE PAYROLL STATUS, which will bring you to the screen shown in Figure 2.

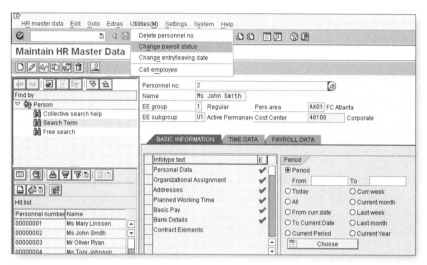

▲ Figure 1 Maintain HR Master Data

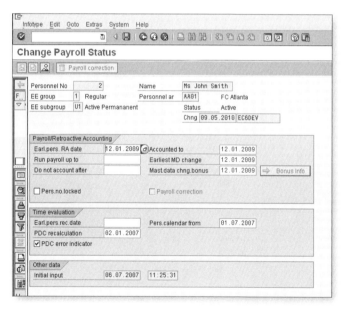

« Figure 2
Change Payroll Status

Change the EARLIEST RETROACTIVE ACCOUNTING DATE or EARLIEST MASTER DATA CHANGES in Infotype 0003 and click Save. Now when you run payroll, the master data record will be picked up to the specified date.

Tip 24: Reversing Your Posting Run Documents

You can easily reverse all incorrectly posted documents for the posting run in question before the bank transfer.

Let's say that the posting documents have been successfully posted for a posting run. The posting status is either documents transferred or documents posted. If you realize your posting is incorrect, you can reverse the posting and create reversal documents. But, they have to be correct, because once the transfer has been executed and sent to the bank, the payments need to be adjusted.

To reverse your posting run, you need to create reversal documents containing all of the document line items for the original documents with reversed plus/minus (+/-) signs. You can then transfer the reversal documents to accounting and post them using standard posting processes. Links to the reversed posting documents are inserted in the reversal documents, which cancels your original posting. Once you have reversed your posting run, you can create a new posting run to repost the corrected payroll results. So, let's get started.

Solution 1

To reverse a posting, take the following steps:

1. Use Transaction PCP040 and navigate to the overview of the posting run, as shown in Figure 1.
2. Select the required posting run. If the posting run containing the posting documents you want to reverse is not displayed, use the following menu path (Figure 1):

> EDIT • FILTER • DELETE FILTER

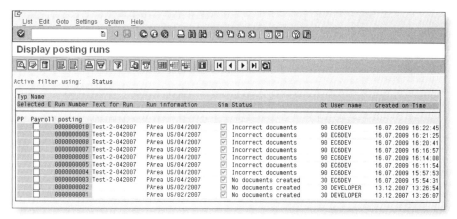

⌃ **Figure 1** Display Posting Run

After selecting the correct posting, use the following menu path (Figure 2):

EDIT • REVERSAL• REVERSAL DOCUMENTS

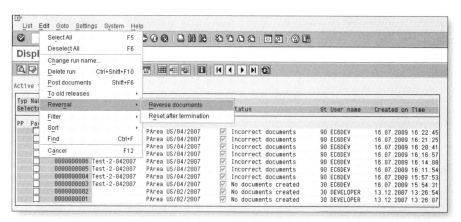

⌃ **Figure 2** Display Posting Run

3. In the dialog box that appears, enter the REVERSAL DATE.

4. Select YES to copy the respective posting date of the original documents as the reversal date. It's important to note, though, that a posting run may contain posting documents with different posting dates.

5. Select NO to enter a different reversal date. If you enter a different posting date, it must be after the posting date for the original documents.

6. To start the reversal, select IMMEDIATELY. You will see a confirmation of the reversal. ∎

Tip 25: Auditing Payroll and Time Schema with Subschemas and PCRs

You can easily review and save your payroll schema by downloading it to Microsoft Excel.

There are several advantages to taking the time to review and edit your schema. The report you use explores the entire schema (to whatever level is chosen), not just the portion relevant to a particular employee. Layout shows the traditional table, with the exact reference to line numbers and subschemas in the output. There are also opportunities for expanded searches, which can help you locate any possible errors in Personal Calculation Rule (PCR) configurations.

You can also choose to display where a particular wage type is being used in the search criteria. The expanded search for a particular wage type will return every possible occurrence of that wage type within the schema. You can review every stage of processing and be aware of possible errors in PCR configurations more easily. You can also save a copy of the output for audit and reference purposes in Microsoft Excel, which we'll discuss in the following solution.

✓ Solution

To display the Payroll and Time Schema and subschemas with PCRs, do the following:

1. Execute report RPDASC00 by using Transaction SE38. Choose the specific selection criteria values (Figure 1).
2. Enter Z<small>NNN</small> for the schema, enter **** to ZZZZ for schemas to be explored, then select E<small>XPAND CALCULATION RULES</small>.
3. Select E<small>XPAND SUBORDINATES</small> PC <small>RULES</small>, then enter **** to ZZZZ for the calculation rules to be expanded.
4. Click Execute, which lets you download the schema output rules to Microsoft Excel (Figure 2).

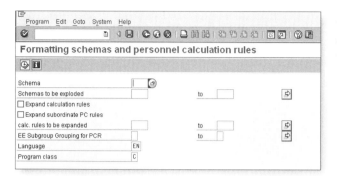

« *Figure 1*
Formatting Schemas and PCRs

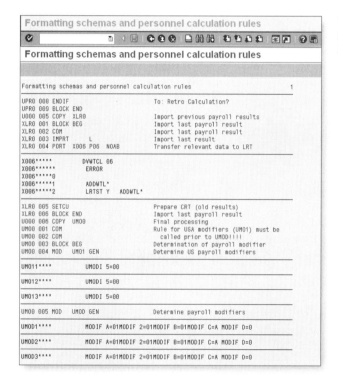

« *Figure 2*
Formatting Schemas and PCRs — Output Rules

You can download the output and save in an Excel spreadsheet via the following menu path:

(LIST • SAVE/SEND • FILE • SPREADSHEET)

With this menu path, you can download output into an Excel spreadsheet using your payroll schema, with subschemas, and PCRs. You can review this document line by line before presenting it for audit and review. ■

Tip 26: Displaying Deleted Payroll Results

You can create an audit process to determine which payroll results have been deleted, by whom, and at what time.

You can easily establish an audit process in your payroll department to monitor and track the deletion of payroll results. In an environment where more than one person may be processing payroll for multiple departments, it's very helpful to create a process that allows you to audit the payroll results and keep track of activity. An audit process will help you to identify payroll issues and errors, and better understand when and why the results were deleted. This level of detail will enable you to implement solutions to reduce or eliminate the issues. So, let's get started.

Solution

The Application Log (Transaction SLG1) is updated with information, such as deleted payroll results, which employee deleted them, and the date they were deleted. You can use Transaction SLG1, or the following menu path, which is shown in Figure 1:

> HUMAN RESOURCES • PAYROLL • AMERICAS • USA • TOOLS • ANALYZE APPLICATION LOG

You can enter the TIME RESTRICTION and OBJECT in the selection screen and click Execute. You will see the output of the DISPLAY LOG, as shown in Figure 2.

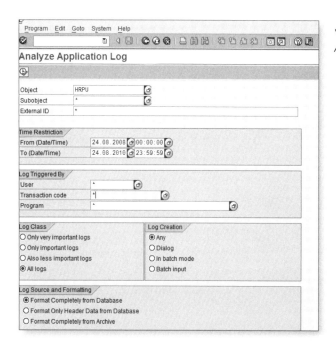

« *Figure 1*
Analyze Application Log

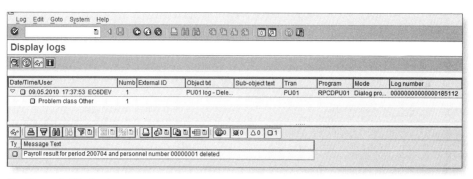

≈ *Figure 2* *Display Logs*

Back in the ANALYZE APPLICATION LOG, you can view which files have been deleted and which employee has done so by entering HRPU in the OBJECT field. In the TIME RESTRICTION box, enter the dates and times to determine the period you want to check, and then click Execute. The result is a list of payroll results deleted during the specified time period. The list also displays the deletion date and the administrator who deleted the payroll results. You can select an entry from the list and choose GOTO to DISPLAY MESSAGES. This will show you additional details for the selected entry. ■

Tip 27 — Inserting Custom Messages in Employee Pay Stubs

You can create custom messages for employees and print the messages on their pay stubs.

If you are running the in-house payroll software in SAP ERP HCM, you can send custom messages to a specific group of employees via their payroll stubs. For example, you could explain certain payments and deductions, changes in payroll contact information, service anniversaries, birthday wishes, and even upcoming events. You can do so by using Infotype 0128 — Notification — during a specific payroll period. Every employee selected to receive a pay stub will receive the message on their pay stub for the pay periods selected.

✓ Solution

You can define additional information in Infotype 0128 that should be printed on your employee's salary/remuneration statement. For example, you can print messages from management or birthday greetings.

Infotype 0128 has the following two subtypes in the standard system:

- **Subtype 1: General notifications**
  You can assign a text module to a personnel number using this subtype. You should have created the text module previously using the function TOOLS • SAPSCRIPT • STANDARD TEXT. You cannot edit the text module directly in Infotype 0128.

  To define additional information, simply go to the following menu path and enter the required data in the TEXT NAME and LANGUAGE fields. In the TEXT ID field, enter HR_G and choose CREATE.

  TOOLS • FORM PRINTOUT • SAP SCRIPT • STANDARD TEXT

Next, choose GOTO • HEADER, and specify a short title for the new text module. You should use a short title for all of the text modules you use. You can get a better overview within Infotype 0128, because the short title, not the text name, is displayed in the list screen or overview screen for the infotype. If you make a change to text module it will affect all of the personnel numbers that the text is assigned to in Infotype 0128.

▶ **Subtype 2: Personal notifications**
Using this subtype, you can edit an individual text module for the personnel number in question. You can only edit and display this text in the infotype.

You can edit personal notifications in Infotype 0128. Using Transaction PA30, you need to create a record for the infotype. Enter the employee's personnel number, select 0128 in the INFOTYPE field and 2 in the SUBTYPE field for a PERSONAL NOTIFICATION, and then choose CREATE. You can enter a short title for the personal notification. At the bottom of the window, you can enter the PERSONAL NOTIFICATION. If this area is too small, you can access the SAPscript editor via MAINTAIN NOTIFICATION. You can now edit the text again and Save when you are done.

Using this subtype, you can edit an individual text module for the personnel. A payroll or HR administrator can create the text for the message directly in the SAP ERP HCM production environment. To display the messages, the pay stub's baseline configuration must be done in the development environment, and then moved to production before you can create the messages.

You can create general text using Transaction S010, and then assign the message to multiple employees. You can access Transaction S010 via the following menu path:

TOOLS • FORM PRINTOUT • SAP SCRIPT • STANDARD TEXT

Select the appropriate LANGUAGE and TEXT ID. You need to use TEXT ID ST (Standard text), as shown in Figure 1. Enter the message TEXT NAME on the main screen; for example, a Happy New Year holiday message. Then click on the Create icon.

The screen that appears, as shown in Figure 1, lets you type in the message you want your employees to see on their pay stubs. Click on Save. Now you can assign the message to a group of employees using the FAST ENTRY screen via Transaction PA70, as shown in Figure 2.

Tip 27 Inserting Custom Messages in Employee Pay Stubs

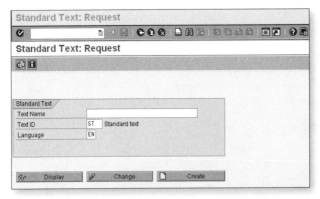

⤒ *Figure 1* Standard Text — Request

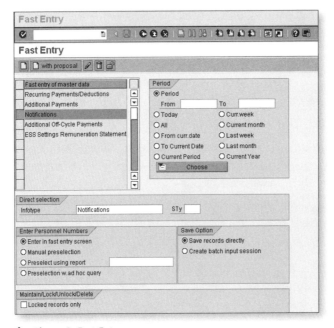

⤒ *Figure 2* Fast Entry

Select Infotype 0128 and then click the ENTER IN FAST ENTRY SCREEN button. Now you can create records for Infotype 0128 for multiple employees with your message. When the payroll is run for the period that has the date or date range in Infotype 0128 record, the chosen messages will appear on the pay stubs. The messages will not be included in payroll runs after the period on Infotype 0128. You can also enter Infotype 0128 via Transaction PA30. As shown in Figure 3, enter the short text title and the text message, and save the record.

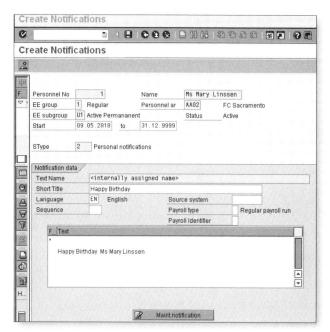

⋀ **Figure 3** *Assign a Personal Message*

You can assign the Infotype 0128 subtype GENERAL NOTIFICATIONS or PERSONAL NOTIFICATIONS to your payroll stub, as shown in Figure 4, and transport it to production after testing.

Sgr	Table	ID	Long text	PTyp	CTy.
1	RT	**02	Print control for payment	01	X
1	RT	**03	Print Control for Time Re	02	X
2	TXT	1	General notifications	05	X

⋀ **Figure 4** *Display Group Layout of Group 01*

Tip 28 — Performing Special and Year-End Adjustments for Payroll

You can manage special and year-end adjustments using Infotype 0221 — Payroll Results Adjustments.

It's not uncommon for businesses to write checks outside of the SAP Payroll system. For example, you may need to provide a terminated employee their last check, or provide an employee with relocation expenses. You can use Infotype 0221 — Payroll Results Adjustments — to perform adjustments that cannot be achieved by regular master data maintenance, such as the following scenarios:

- Entering manual checks in SAP, written outside of SAP ERP HCM
- Creating payroll results where the taxed-when-earned method is applied
- Performing year-end adjustments via the year-end adjustments workbench

The data from checks written outside of SAP ERP HCM must be entered into the system to ensure correct year-to-date (YTD) calculations, consistency in reconciliation, and employee W2s that accurately reflect their taxable income.

 ## Solution

To carry out special adjustments, you can enter the wage types as an amount in Infotype 0221, and tax wage types to the appropriate tax authorities. You can specify up to 20 wage types per Infotype 0221 record with certain restrictions. By default, Infotype 0221 amounts are assigned to the employee's tax company and tax authorities for the defined adjustment date entered on the infotype. The system, however, allows you to perform a tax company override or you can assign all wage types to a different work tax area, residence tax area, or unemployment tax authority.

You can also assign the wage type amounts of Infotype 0221 to different cost object, such as a business area or cost center. In payroll, wage types entered in Infotype 0221 are assigned to the home cost center defined in the Infotype 0001 — Organizational Assignment. If you choose to assign a different cost object, all wage type amounts will be assigned to this cost object.

Changes to the last payroll result of a previous year are processed by means of year-end adjustments. You can access the year-end adjustments workbench using Transaction PA30 or via the following menu path:

> PAYROLL • USA • SUBSEQUENT ACTIVITIES • PERIOD INDEPENDENT • PAYROLL SUPPLEMENT (SPECIAL RETRO PROCESSING)

This workbench facilitates the process of creating year-end adjustments and enables users to distinguish between the two available kinds of year-end adjustments: Subtype YAWA (with tax calculation) and Subtype YANA (without tax calculation).

There is no restriction on the net amount of subtype YANA adjustments, and these adjustments can be positive or negative. Subtype YANA adjustments will cause a new final payroll result to be created for the prior year.

A significant advantage of the year-end adjustment process under subtype YANA is that adjustments and master data changes won't affect the year-end adjustment process, and vice versa. This functionality enables an extended period to check and reconcile year-end adjustment data. Furthermore, the year-end adjustment payroll run will only contain data for the corresponding year-end adjustment.

When processing for YANA is complete, the system creates a special payroll result that contains all adjustment data in results table RT for the affected payroll period. This result will also update YTD amounts in tables CRT and TCRT.

Because year-end adjustments entered on subtype YANA in Infotype 0221 are not considered by regular payroll runs, you may enter and reconcile data for year-end adjustments over an extended period of time, before you ultimately perform the payroll run for the adjustment. The year-end adjustment payroll run will only contain amounts that were created in Infotype 0221, as shown in Figure 1.

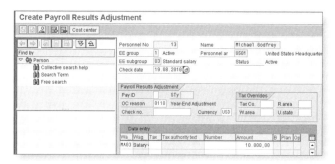

⌃ *Figure 1* Create Payroll Results Adjustments

Tip 29: Updating Payroll Schemas and PCRs with Line Editor Commands

You can maintain complex payroll schemas and Personal Calculation Rules (PCRs) easily and efficiently by using line commands and functions.

Most administrators are not frequent users of payroll schemas, but do have to maintain them from time to time. Schema maintenance is a complex process, and it can be quite cumbersome to update them without knowing line commands and functions.

 Solution

Line commands allow you to move, delete, copy, and insert a line. You can use the following most common line editor commands to maintain schemas:

- D: Deletes a line
- I: Inserts a line
- M: Moves a line
- C: Copies a line
- DD: Indicates the start of a block to be deleted
- DD: Indicates the end of a block to be copied
- CC: Indicates the start of a block to be copied
- CC: Indicates the end of a block to be copied
- MM: Indicates the start of a block to be moved
- MM: Indicates the end of a block to be moved

Once you choose a block to be moved or copied, you need to specify where the block should move to within the schema. You do this using either of the following line commands:

- A: Places the block after the chosen line
- B: Places the block before the chosen line

The following are commonly used functions used to maintain schemas:

- Copy: Calls a schema placed in PAR1
- Block: Defines the start and end of a nested node
- PRT: Processes the Results Table
- PIT: Processes the Input Table
- IF/ELSE: Processes the schema if the condition is fulfilled
- ACTIO: Calls a PCR

To maintain your SAP ERP HCM payroll schemas and PCRs using line commands, use the following menu path:

> HUMAN RESOURCES • PAYROLL• AMERICAS • USA • TOOLS • CUSTOMIZING TOOLS • PE01 SCHEMA

Select the schema you want to update, as shown in Figure 1, and apply the line commands and functions for maintaining the schema. To access the schema, double-click on a subschema to take you to the maintenance screen for that schema.

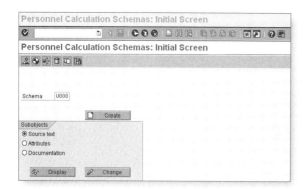

« Figure 1
Personnel Calculation Schemas — Initial Screen

Double-click on any of the rules, you will be brought to the rule editor. By looking at the parameters, you can differentiate between a subschema and a PCR. You can call a subschema by using the COPY command. You can use the line commands listed previously to move, insert, delete, or copy a line. For letter commands, type the letter(s) and press Enter. For example, if you wish to delete a line, type the line command D and press Enter.

Tip 30: Creating Files for Third Party Providers

Instead of investing in a custom interface or program to send master or payroll data to a third-party provider, you can use the HR Interface Toolbox PU12 in SAP ERP HCM.

If your company doesn't run payroll in-house, you'll need to export HR master data from the personnel administration, payroll, and time management components to your third-party provider. You can use HR Toolbox PU12 to configure a basic SAP export file. By default, Transaction PU12 creates and transfers data in a plain-text file, which can be exported to third-party providers via FTP, email (with encryption), or other methods your company may use.

✓ Solution

You can use Toolbox PU12 to export data to third-party providers. You can export master, time, and payroll data by country (if necessary) when using this tool. You can select both the infotypes and fields you want to see and specify the layout of the export file. To get to the tool, navigate the following menu path:

> HUMAN RESOURCES • PAYROLL • AMERICAS • USA • TOOLS • OUTSOURCING-INTERFACE TOOLBOX • PU12 INTERFACE TOOLBOX

Click Execute, which will bring you to the INTERFACE TOOLBOX, as shown in Figure 1.

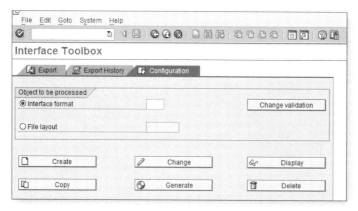

⚐ *Figure 1* Interface Toolbox

As you can see, there are three tabs in the INTERFACE TOOLBOX:

- EXPORT: Displays the results from running the export
- EXPORT HISTORY: Displays the log and results of previously executed runs
- CONFIGURATION: Configures the format of your interface per third-party file layout requirements for exports

    Within the CONFIGURATION tab, there are two layout options:

    - The INTERFACE FORMAT allows you to specify the selection/input layout of the interface.
    - The FILE LAYOUT enables you to configure the layout to specify the output of the interface.

    Ideally, you need to generate the interface format and file layout every time you make a change in any of them, so that it generates fresh ABAP code for the configuration and does not generate errors.

Next, configure the system with the following steps to determine the data available in the output:

1. In the CREATE INTERFACE FORMAT screen, enter an INTERFACE FORMAT and select the country, then export the file.
2. Specify which data to export (either MASTER DATA or PAYROLL RESULTS/TIME DATA).
3. Select the infotypes that you want to include in the export, as shown in Figure 2.

Tip 30 Creating Files for Third Party Providers

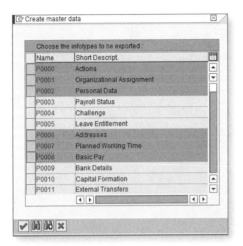

« *Figure 2*
Create Master Data

4. Change the INTERFACE FORMAT TEST: DATA SELECTION by selecting the fields you want included in the export file, as shown in Figure 3.

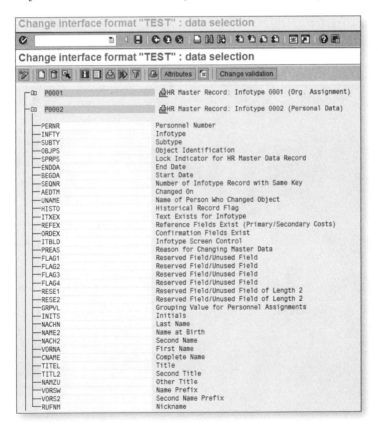

« *Figure 3*
Change Interface Format

5. With the entries shown in Figure 4, you can control which of the infotype's records the export program processes. SAP recommends leaving the defaults, which, in this case, is ALL RECORDS VALID ON AT LEAST ONE DAY OF THE CURRENT PERIOD.

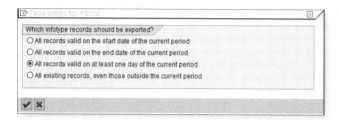

« **Figure 4**
Table Entries for P0002

6. Now you can change the INTERFACE FORMAT TEST to the data selection, which lets you link the PU12 export program and file layout conversion process as a single executable program.

7. Finally, enter the selection criteria for your interface program and click Execute. This will generate the export file, which you can save and send to your third party (see Figure 5).

« **Figure 5**
Export File

Tip 31 — Deleting Current Payroll Results for an Employee

If the payroll was run incorrectly or by mistake, you can delete current payroll results for an employee.

There are a number of possible situations in which payroll may have been run incorrectly for an employee or group of employees. One scenario is that the employee shouldn't have been included in the payroll run because he is on unpaid leave. You can correct the situation by deleting the current payroll results after the payroll run has been completed for the employee in question. Once you have deleted the payroll results, you can run the payroll again correctly.

When using this process, however, you can only delete payroll results for the last payroll. So, let's get started.

Solution

Program RPCDPU01 contains all of the modules for Transaction PU01. This transaction lets you specify a personnel number within the current payroll result to be deleted from cluster Rx (x stands for the country grouping) in database table PCL2. Once the DELETE button is clicked, the system automatically performs the following activities:

- Deletes current payroll results and previous payroll results become the current payroll results.
- Updates Infotype 0003 — Payroll Status.
- Updates the Application Log (Transaction SLG1) with the deleted payroll result. This log records the deleted payroll, the date, and the user ID of whoever deleted it.

To get to program RPCDPU01, use the following menu path:

> PAYROLL • AMERICAS • USA • TOOLS • PROBLEM SOLVING • DELETE PAYROLL RESULTS

Click Execute, which will bring you to the screen shown in Figure 1.

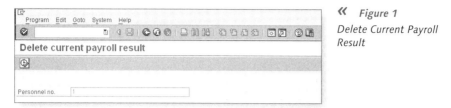

« *Figure 1*
Delete Current Payroll Result

Here, you can enter the personnel number of the employee's payroll result that you want to delete. Click Execute, and you will see the screen shown in Figure 2.

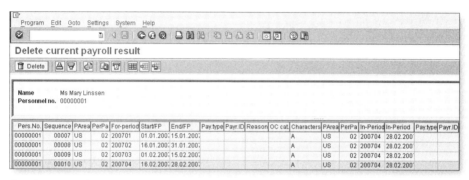

⩓ *Figure 2* *Delete Current Payroll Results*

On this screen, you can select the payroll result you want to delete and click on the DELETE button. You will see the pop-up message, "If you delete the current payroll result, this data will be irretrievably lost. Do you still want to delete?" Select YES. You will receive a confirmation that the payroll results for the employee you selected were deleted, as shown in Figure 3.

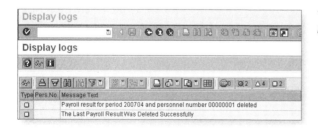

« *Figure 3*
Display Log

Part 5

Time Management

Things You'll Learn in this Section

32	Using Report RPUSWH00 for Infotype 0007 — Mass Update	92
33	Troubleshooting Payroll and Time-Related Issues and Displaying Time Evaluation Results	96
34	Generating Automatic Absence Quotas	100
35	Checking Attendance and Absence Types	102
36	Displaying the Personnel Work Schedule for Multiple Employees for a Given Period	106
37	Displaying and Changing Your Holiday Calendar	110
38	Simplifying Your SAP Time Evaluation Schema	114
39	Reviewing the Error Log Generated During Time Evaluation	116
40	Correcting Absence Quotas Generated in Time Evaluation	118

Time Management supports Human Resources (HR) processes involving the planning, recording, valuation of work, and absence times. It provides data and information to other business applications and processes. It is flexible enough to support centralized or decentralized administration, entry and processing of data online, or using self-service applications. Employees can request leave, record working times, and display their key time accounts. It also allows you to represent any company agreements, collective agreement stipulations, or legal requirements. This section of tips will help the developers, business analysts, system administrators, and functional power-users who are focused in SAP ERP HCM to streamline time management processes and data administration.

Tip 32 Using Report RPUSWH00 for Infotype 0007 — Mass Update

You can easily use Infotype 0007 — Mass Update — to update records for multiple employees using a standard report.

Let's say your company completed contract negotiations with your unions and the annual work hours for employees changed from 2000 to 2080 hours. Now you have to update the work schedule with the new effective dates to show the correct daily, weekly, monthly, and annual hours. The work schedule is assigned to an employee in Infotype 0007.

Making the change to the work schedule in the configuration doesn't automatically apply the change to all impacted employees. In this example, there are 3,000 employees who will be impacted. So, you need to use Infotype 0007. By using the standard delivered Revaluation of Planned Working Times report (RPUWSH00), you can ensure that all of the changes made in the configuration for the existing work schedule are updated easily and quickly in Infotype 0007 for the employees.

 Solution

To maintain the time evaluation and payroll run data in Infotype 0007 correctly, you should use report RPUWSH00 for work schedule rule changes. This report shows which planned working time records (Infotype 0007) feature a work schedule rule, employment percentage, and fields that are different from the new work schedule rule. Infotype 0007 records will be copied and delimited, and you can process records based on the selection screen directly, or in a batch input session. To get to Infotype 0007, use the following menu path:

HUMAN RESOURCES • TIME MANAGEMENT • ADMINISTRATION • TOOLS • TOOLS
SELECTION • WORK SCHEDULE • REVALUATE PLANNED WORKING TIME

You will see the selection screen shown in Figure 1. Enter the personnel number or range of personnel numbers, and the selections for the WORK SCHEDULE RULE that has been changed. This WORK SCHEDULE RULE will be used to insert a new record in Infotype 0007 for all of the employees you select (Figure 1).

« *Figure 1*
Revaluation of Planned Working Time

On this screen, enter the values in the selection criteria and execute the report. Because the TEST RUN checkbox is checked, Infotype 0007 won't be updated this time. You can see the results in Figure 2.

Once you execute this report, it will delimit the old record and insert a new Infotype 0007 record. To check, use Transaction PA20 and select a few employee numbers to see that the change has been done.

Tip 32   Using Report RPUSWH00 for Infotype 0007 — Mass Update

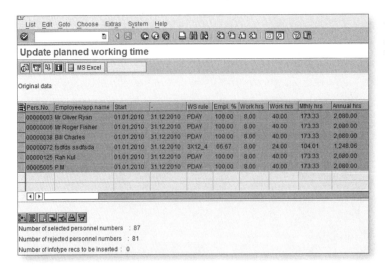

« Figure 2
Update Planned Working Time

Here, you can see the results of the test run. To generate the final results, uncheck the TEST RUN box in the selection screen in Figure 1 and click EXECUTE again. You can see the updated Infotype 0007 records in Figure 3. If it's easier, you can run this program in the background.

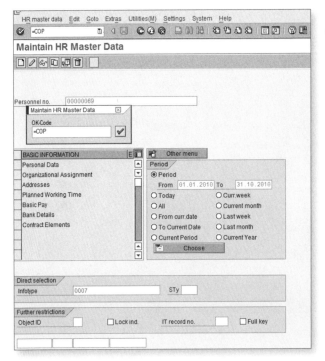

« Figure 3
Maintain HR Master Data

A new record is created. You have successfully mass updated the Infotype 0007 record for multiple employees with the new work schedule, as shown in Figure 4.

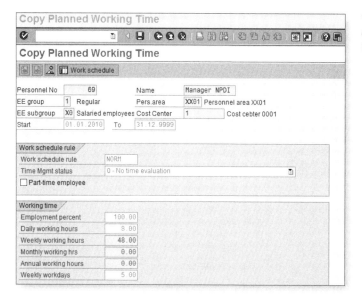

« *Figure 4*
Copy Planned Working Time

Tip 33 — Troubleshooting Payroll and Time-Related Issues and Displaying Time Evaluation Results

After running Time Evaluation, you can review the results for each employee to troubleshoot any time or payroll issues or inquiries.

After completing Time Evaluation, your payroll administer reviews the error log and resolves any time issues. You or your payroll administrator can view the results for each employee stored in the Time Management functionality of SAP ERP HCM using structures called B2 clusters (or clusters, for short). You can view B2 clusters and report on them using Transaction PT66. You can report on the B2 cluster Time Evaluation period, which is typically one month. For example, January is period 1, February is period 2, and so on. The stored B2 cluster results include wage types, quota accruals, attendance, absences, current actions, time evaluation messages, and substitutions. This report can be used to troubleshoot payroll and time-related inquiries.

The clusters in file PCL2 are permanent. Data remains in B2 clusters until the clusters are reorganized. This lets you view all of the data ever recorded and processed for an employee and to repeat time evaluation runs for testing purposes. Evaluations are based on the data in B2 clusters. Some examples of the tables stored in the B2 clusters are: WPBP (Basic Pay), SALDO (Cumulated Time Balances), ZL (time Wage Types), and C1 (Cost Distribution). You may have to troubleshoot incorrect values or errors using the following solution.

✓ Solution

Once you have completed the Time Evaluation, the results are saved to various tables. The Time Evaluation results include: time balances, time wage types, data for updating infotypes (for example, time quotas), and messages from time evaluation. You can use the results to perform other tasks, such as passing the results to payroll or including them as input for the next Time Evaluation run. The results can be used for reporting (the time statement, for example) and for evaluations. After Time Evaluation processing, the results are stored in the tables in the B1 and B2 clusters. All Time Evaluation results (cumulated balances, time wage types, messages, etc.) are stored for individual employees and periods in the B2 cluster. The B2 cluster is used to maintain a history of time data. In the B1 cluster, you will see the time balances that are read to download to the time recording system.

Any special situations or missing data during Time Evaluation could result in errors. You can run Transaction PT66 to display the current content of B2 clusters. There are two levels of lists available to display, and they can be set in the selection screen:

- The first level is a list of personnel numbers, where you can see an overview of selected personnel numbers. You can see an overview of the tables in a B2 cluster containing information about the number of entries created. If you choose to display detailed information about all tables, you can display a list of all entries in all tables. This function is useful if you want to print the list to analyze errors in more detail.
- The second level is a detailed description of all table entries. You can select this option to display all table functions that you can access from the list of personnel numbers. The system displays the entries in the individual tables for all selected employees.

To get to the screen with these options (Figure 1), use Transaction PT66 or the following menu path:

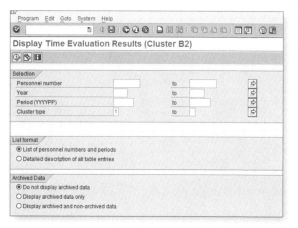

« *Figure 1*
Display Time Evaluation Results (B2 Cluster)

Tip 33 Troubleshooting Payroll and Time-Related Issues and Displaying Time Evaluation Results

> HUMAN RESOURCES • TIME MANAGEMENT • ADMINISTRATION • TOOLS • TOOL SELECTION • CLUSTER • PT_CLSTB2

Click on the Execute button and you will see the DISPLAY TIME EVALUATION RESULTS screen, as shown in Figure 2.

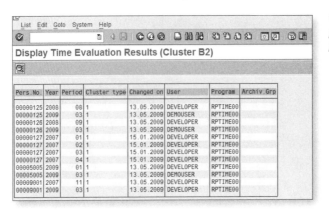

« **Figure 2**
Display Time Evaluation Results

To see the Time Evaluation RESULTS for selected employees, go to the screen in Figure 1 and select LIST OF PERSONNEL NUMBER AND PERIODS. You can see the output in Figure 3.

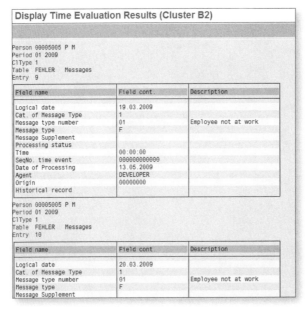

« **Figure 3**
Display Time Evaluation Results (Cluster B2)

As you can see, the results of the Time Evaluation for selected employees with the detail description option of all table entries are shown here, and it includes results for each employee.

Figure 4 displays the results of Time Evaluation for selected employees with the detail description option for all table entries selected. In addition, you can see the results for each employee. You can now review the results and troubleshoot the payroll or employee times.

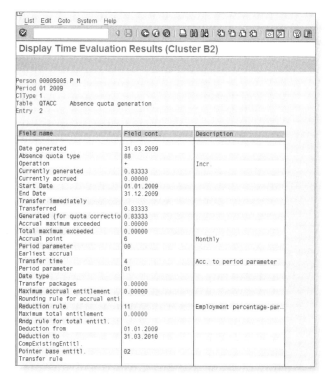

« *Figure 4*

Display Time Evaluation Results (Cluster B2) — Detailed Description

Tip 34 Generating Automatic Absence Quotas

Even if you are not using Time Evaluation in SAP ERP HCM, you can still generate and save absence quotas for employees.

You can generate absence quotas using report RPTQTA00 regardless of whether you're using Time Evaluation in SAP ERP HCM. The absences are saved as records of absence quotas in Infotype 2006. The automatic nature of this report is helpful in adding time-off entitlements for both individuals and groups of employees. You can generate different quota numbers based on organizational assignment, age, or seniority of the employee. This report, however, cannot handle scenarios as complex as those that can be done in Time Evaluation.

Solution

The report RPTQTA00 generates time-off entitlements for a defined generation interval. The generation interval determines the validity period of the absence quota record being created. You can enter the start and end date of the quota directly using the other period field on the selection screen shown in Figure 1. The date is used as the key date for determining the actual validity interval according to the validity period.

There are three ways to generate the records. You can choose one of the following options and run the report to generate the absence quotas and update Infotype 2006.

- **Batch Input:** By selecting this option, a batch input processing session is generated during the program run and can be processed later.
- **Directly:** By selecting this option, new or changed infotype records are updated directly.
- **Test Mode:** By selecting this option, you can run the report in test mode and review the results before they are transferred to Infotype 2006.

You can use Transaction SE38 to get these options.

From here, you can enter RPTQTA00 in the selection field and click Execute, which brings you to the screen shown in Figure 1.

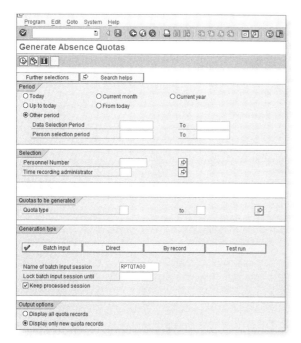

« *Figure 1*
Generating Absence Quotas

Enter the PERSONNEL NUMBER and TIME RECORDING ADMINISTRATOR values in the SELECTION section, and the QUOTA TYPE for your company. Click on the Execute icon, which will bring you to the output screen shown in Figure 2.

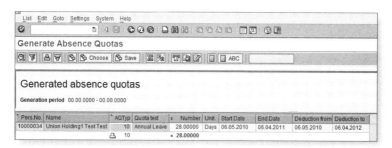

˄ *Figure 2* Generated Absence Quotas

As you can see, this screen displays the results of the ABSENCE QUOTAS and provides you with a list of records for absence quotas.

Tip 35 Checking Attendance and Absence Types

You can use report RPT55400 to create a list of all attendance and absence types set up in SAP ERP HCM.

It is very important to have the correct accurate values (per company policies) for your attendance, absence types for employee time to be evaluated and paid correctly and accurately.

This requires you to know the different attendance and absence types set up in your SAP ERP HCM system, and the values for each type, such as absence input checks (minimum and maximum duration of absences). Using report RPT55400, you can determine the absence calendar control values for a given absence type. This level of detail will help you audit your time data against current company policies for absences and vacations and keep your system in compliance.

Absence and attendance types can have a major impact on the enterprise, as they both affect how employees are paid. For example, absences such as leave or time off from work affects how employees are paid and how time is evaluated during absences and on statistics and evaluations. The same is true for attendance. Definitions of your attendance types depend on the policies and processes your company has adopted for recording time. You use a separate attendance type to record each type of attendance that has an independent meaning and is to be specially processed. For example, you want to document special employee attendance times (such as overtime, works council activities, or work from home).

Once you've set up attendances and absence types in customization, you can periodically review them using report RPT55400. This will help you determine if you need to make changes to your existing values for your attendance or absence types or configure new attendance or absence types in customization.

Solution

The Time Management functionality contains the Infotype 2002 (Attendance) and Infotype 2001 (Absences). You can define company-specific attendance types, absence types, and reasons for the infotypes. You can create specific attendance and absence types for your enterprise in customization in the IMG. You can track and monitor the Attendance and Absence types you created using report RPT55400. This report provides an overview of Attendance/Absences types from table T554S, including the following details:

- Personnel Subarea Grouping (PSG)
- Attendance/Absence Type (A/AType)
- Attendance/Absence Type Text
- Start/End Date of the Attendance/Absence Type
- Minimum and Maximum Absence Allowed

You can drill down into more details by selecting a line item and clicking on the Detail icon. The results can be downloaded to an Excel spreadsheet for further analysis or sharing. You can review and maintain accurate values for your Attendance and Absence types. The correct values are a prerequisite for accurate use of the Time Data Recording and Administration component

To get to table T554S, use the following menu path:

> TIME MANAGEMENT • ADMINISTRATION • TOOLS • TOOLS SELECTION • PT_55400 FIND ATTENDANCE/ABSENCE.

Enter the values in the selection criteria as shown in Figure 1, and click on the Execute icon.

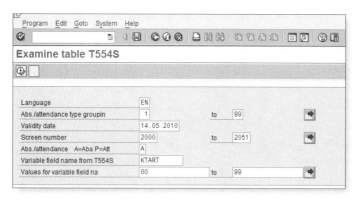

« *Figure 1*
Examine Table T554S

Tip 35 Checking Attendance and Absence Types

In this example, all the absence types for this organization will be displayed because we entered A for ABSENCE. (Entering P for Attendance would have returned all the Attendance types for display.) Click on the Execute icon, which will bring you to the output screen, as shown in Figure 2.

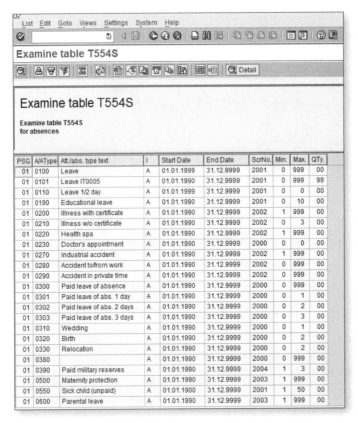

« *Figure 2*
Absence Types Output Screen

Figure 2 displays the list of absence types. Select the Absence Type (A/A TYPE) that you want to review or update, and click on the Detail icon. This will bring you to the screen shown in Figure 3.

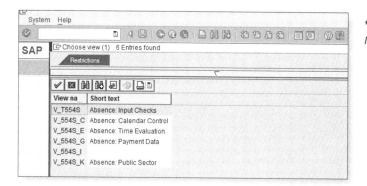

« *Figure 3*
Restrictions

From here, you can select a line item. In this example, we've chosen ABSENCE: INPUT CHECKS. Once you select a line item, you will be brought to the details screen shown in Figure 4.

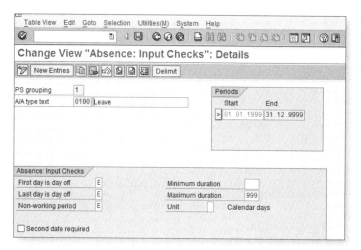

« *Figure 4*
*Change View —
Absence: Input
Checks Detail*

Here, you can review the details and make changes, if needed. It's important to remember to make all of the changes in your development environment, test them, and then move your changes to production. Once you've done this, you've successfully reviewed the entries in table T554S for Attendance/Absence types. ■

Tip 36: Displaying the Personnel Work Schedule for Multiple Employees for a Given Period

You can create and display an overview of working times and rules for your employees during any given period. You can also include the attendance records in the output for any given period.

You can display an overview of the personal work schedules for multiple employees for any given period. This overview can include all essential details about the working time of an employee. You can display a list to see if the time infotype records were entered for an employee on a particular day. Detailed information on these employee time infotype records, daily work schedules, and planned working time is available, and the results can be downloaded into a spreadsheet for future reference. You can easily review, analyze, and audit the data from the spreadsheet. You can review all attendance types and flag any discrepancies. You can also use and share this report with your Payroll department or third-party providers as needed.

 Solution

Once you've executed report RPTSH10, you can retrieve the following details from the report:

- **Information on Daily Work Schedule (DSW):** You can select the DSW to view details about the daily work schedule of an employee.
- **Information on Planned Working Time:** You can display the Details screen for Infotype 0007 — Planned Working Time — by selecting a line in the list. This will display detailed information on planned working time.

▶ **Information on Time Infotypes:** You can display an overview of all of the Time infotype records that were recorded on selected days.

You can get this report in an interactive list where you can view the details of several time infotype records, including, Attendance (Infotype 2001), Absences (Infotype 2002), Substitutions (Infotype 2003), Availability (Infotype 2004), and Overtime (Infotype 2005). You can also view detailed information on daily work schedules or planned working time (Infotype 0007). The report also lists any errors (such as those occurring in Customizing). The list displays error messages with personnel numbers.

From the output list you can see the daily work schedule for planned working time and you can see detailed information on time infotypes.

Enter RPTPSH10 in the SELECTION field, and click on the Execute icon. This will display the selection screen shown in Figure 1.

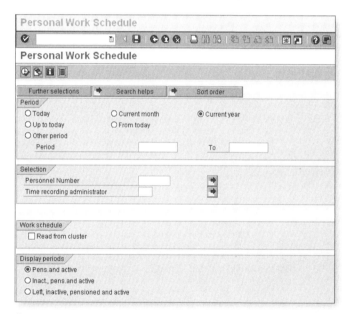

⌃ *Figure 1 Personnel Work Schedule*

Tip 36 *Displaying the Personnel Work Schedule for Multiple Employees for a Given Period*

Enter the personnel numbers of the employees you want to run this report for and click the Execute icon. You will see the work schedule details as shown in Figure 2.

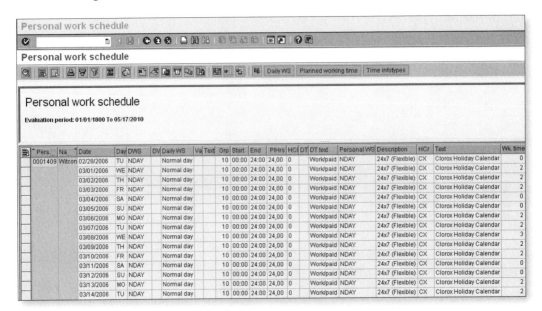

⌃ *Figure 2 Personal Work Schedule*

This screen displays the output for the multiple employees report.

To display detailed information on the daily work schedule, select a line on the daily work schedule, and then select DWS (daily work schedule). The DISPLAY DAILY WORK SCHEDULE: OVERVIEW screen appears.

To display detailed information on planned working time, select the lines in the planned working time, and then choose Planned working time. The screen for Infotype 0007 appears for the first line you select.

To get to this report, use Transaction SE38 and enter report RPTPSH10.

You can select a line item and click on the TIME INFOTYPES button to display the time infotypes, which brings you to the screen shown in Figure 3.

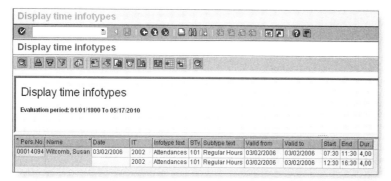

⌃ **Figure 3** Display Time Infotypes

You can see Infotype 0007 in Figure 4.

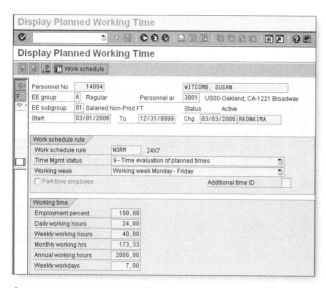

⌃ **Figure 4** Display Planned Working Time

Once you've completed this, you've successfully created an overview of work schedules and time infotypes for one or more employees. ■

Tip 37: Displaying and Changing Your Holiday Calendar

Using Transaction SCAL, you can display and maintain your company's SAP ERP HCM holiday calendar, public calendar, and factory calendar. This allows you to periodically review the calendars to maintain their accuracy and stay compliant with company policies.

You can generate and review a list of your company holiday calendars in SAP ERP HCM using Transaction SCAL. This transaction provides an overview of the public, holiday, and factory calendars, and the ability to drill down to see their details.

Holiday calendars are the baseline calendars used for time management and payroll calculations. It's common practice to update holiday calendars annually, which is often done in December for the following year.

Just changing the holiday calendar is not sufficient, however, because these changes are not automatically reflected on your work schedule and time infotypes, such as Planned Working Time (Infotype 0007), Attendances (Infotype 2002), Absences (Infotype 2001), and the annual calendar, monthly calendar, and weekly calendar. By just changing the holiday calendar, you're also missing an opportunity to calculate absence quotas correctly in Infotype 2006. You will have to regenerate your work schedule through Transaction PT01 and then run report RPTUPD00 to fix any discrepancies, which we'll discuss in the following solution.

Solution

To display or change your holiday calendar, you can use Transaction SCAL or go to the following menu path. The calendar is not client specific. Each change made takes effect directly in all clients.

HUMAN RESOURCES • TIME MANAGEMENT • ADMINISTRATION • WORK SCHEDULE • HOLIDAY CALENDAR

Click on HOLIDAY CALENDAR, which will bring you to the screen shown in Figure 1.

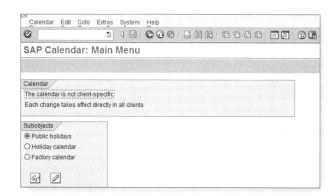

« *Figure 1*
SAP Calendar: Main Menu

From here, click the HOLIDAY DISPLAY button, and then click on the Display icon, which brings you to the screen shown in Figure 2.

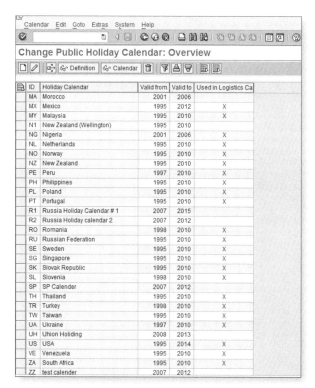

« *Figure 2*
Change Public Holiday Calendar: Overview

Tip 37 Displaying and Changing Your Holiday Calendar

This overview screen shows a list of Holiday Calendars configured in the SAP ERP HCM System. Select the HOLIDAY CALENDAR you want to review and update, and then click on the Change icon. This will bring you to the screen shown in Figure 3.

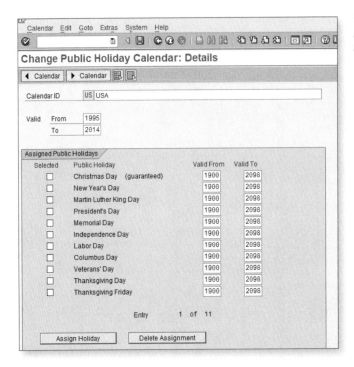

« Figure 3
Change Public Holiday Calendar: Details

You can review the list for accuracy. To make changes and maintain holiday calendars, you need to navigate to the SAP CALENDAR MENU screen and click on CHANGE. You can edit the values in your holiday calendar and Save it (see Figure 4).

In this example, you've reviewed the Holiday Calendar and learned how to update and save your entries as needed.

It's important to keep in mind that these changes are not cascaded everywhere automatically. You'll need to perform the follow-up steps listed below to reflect the changes in the work schedule and time infotypes and the weekly, monthly, and annual calendars:

- After assigning a new date to the holiday in the calendar, you can generate the work schedule using Transaction PT01.
- Run report RPTUPD00 to fix discrepancies among Infotypes 0007, 2001, 2002, and 2006.

Be sure to make the changes in your development system first and then move them to production.

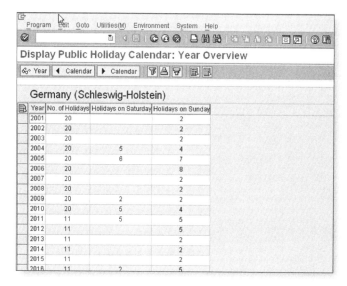

« *Figure 4*
Public Holiday Calendar with List of Holidays

Tip 38: Simplifying Your SAP Time Evaluation Schema

Company policy and business rules related to time and pay are often complex. Translating them accurately into SAP Time Evaluation Schema and Personnel Calculation Rules (PCRs) is easy when you use standard SAP operations.

You can simplify and apply your company's time and pay policies, and the business rules to your SAP Time Evaluation Schema and PCRs, using standard SAP functions and time schema parameters. For example, you can use the master data fields to simplify and implement policies based on multiple criteria in your time schemas. You can use these infotype values to control the Comp Time Payout. You can specify the rules in operation OUTWP to define when the Comp Time is paid out. Operation OUTWP provides work center data to the variable key. This operation can use values from infotypes mentioned earlier to trigger rules in time evaluation processing.

The following is a list of some of the employee data in Infotype 001 — Organizational Assignment — that can be used to apply policies and business rules in your time schema using operation OUTWP.

- PLANT: Personnel Area
- PLTSC: Personnel Subarea
- COSTC: Cost Center
- GSBER: Business Area
- PERSG: Employee Group
- PERSB: Employee Subgroup
- PAYSB: Payroll Area
- PLANS: Position Key

- JOBNO: Job Key
- VDSK1: Org Key
- MOLGA: Country Grouping
- EXMPT: Exempt (Y/N)
- COMPY: Company Code

Solution

You can update your schema and PCRs using the parameters and functions available in SAP ERP HCM. You can write your rules using the Master Data fields in Infotypes 0000 (Actions), 0001, 0002 (Personnel Data), 007 (Planned Working Time), and 0008 (Basic Pay). To start off, navigate to the following menu path:

> HUMAN RESOURCES • TIME MANAGEMENT • TOOLS • PE01 • MAINTAIN SCHEMAS

To modify your schema, enter the name of the schema in the selection field and click on CHANGE. You can also use the copy function to create a copy of your schema to test your changes. You'll see the schema screen shown in Figure 1.

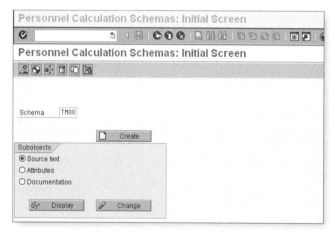

« *Figure 1*
Personnel Calculation Schemas — Initial Screen

You can make changes to your PCRs and apply operation OUTWP to your decision trees to effectively apply company time, pay policies, and business rules. ■

Tip 39 — Reviewing the Error Log Generated During Time Evaluation

You can review the error log generated during Time Evaluation after report RPTIME00 has been run for a chosen day.

Once Time Evaluation has been run, it is important for your time administrator to review the error log and messages so that all errors can be fixed and all employee time data can be processed accurately. It's important to review the error log generated during the Time Evaluation process. You can do this through Transaction PT_ERL00. It's a good practice to run this report on a weekly basis or after completing your time evaluation run for all employees. This report will generate a detailed list of error messages that can be reviewed and researched further. You can also download and save the list in an Excel spreadsheet.

Solution

The messages (error number and error long text) are identified by the following colors:

- Grey: the message has a note
- Light Red: the message has a recalculation
- Dark Red: the message indicates that time evaluation was terminated

To get to the time evaluation messages, use the following menu path:

> HUMAN RESOURCES • TIME MANAGEMENT • ADMINISTRATION • TIME EVALUATION • PT_ERL00 –TIME EVALUATION MESSAGES

Click on the report and you will see the selection screen shown in Figure 1. Enter the selection criteria.

Choose OTHER PERIOD in the period and enter the period dates. Click Execute, which will bring you to the screen shown in Figure 2.

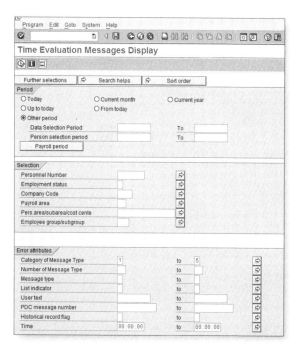

« **Figure 1**
Time Evaluation Messages — Selection Criteria

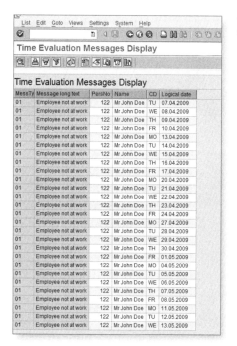

« **Figure 2**
Time Evaluation Message Display

You can also run this report for a specific employee by selecting the personnel number (PER NO) in the selection screen. ∎

Tip 40 Correcting Absence Quotas Generated in Time Evaluation

After generating Absence Quota records, you may need to correct a few individual records by adjusting their quota entitlement.

The need to adjust Absence Quota records is not uncommon. For example, let's say you have an employee who has recently joined your company. The new employee's offer includes 13 extra days of absence entitlement as compensation for the balance of vacation they left behind at the other company (for the current year). In this example, you would want to set the employee's starting absence quota balance to a fixed value of 13 days. Another example would be after running Time Evaluation in SAP ERP HCM, you notice that too much absence entitlement has been generated for an employee due to incorrect master data.

You can use the Quota Overview to correct an employee's absence entitlements. You can use two different processes for quota corrections depending on how the absence entitlements were created: If your absence entitlements were created manually, you should use the Absence Quotas in Infotype 2006, where you can make the corrections manually. If you generated time evaluations, and you want to enter a correction for a quota, you could use Infotype 2013. The correction is made the next time Time Evaluation is run. On the ABSENCE QUOTAS tab, you can check the DET. ENT. field (indicator for determining quota entitlement) to see if the entitlement was entered manually or automatically. However, some quotas do not permit manual corrections. For such quotas, you can only transfer the entitlement generated by time evaluation directly to Infotype 2006.

✓ Solution

You can use Infotype 2006 to correct Absence Quotas if you are using Time Evaluation in SAP ERP HCM. The changes are taken into account during the next Time Evaluation run. Time Evaluation performs a recalculation starting on the day you entered for the quota correction. To get to Infotype 2006, use the following menu path:

> HUMAN RESOURCES • TIME MANAGEMENT • ADMINISTRATION • TIME DATA •
> QUOTA OVERVIEW

This is where you can select the Absence Quota record that you want to correct. To correct absence entitlements entered manually, you need to select the relevant personnel number and choose the required selection intervals. You then choose ABSENCE QUOTAS and then select EXPAND. You will see an overview of all of the employee's existing absence quotas (see Figure 1). You can select the absence quota you want to correct by clicking CHANGE ENTITLEMENT. When Infotype 2006 appears, you can make the required changes and save.

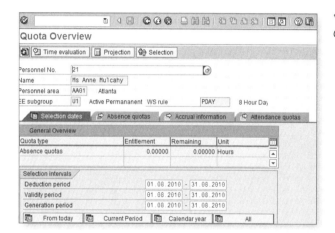

« *Figure 1*
Quota Overview

Follow the steps as described previously and be sure to click Save. You have now corrected an employee's Absence Quota record (see Figure 2).

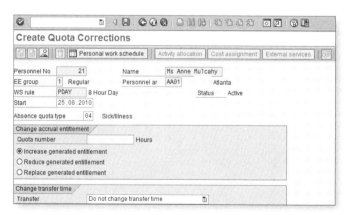

« *Figure 2*
Create Quota Correction

Part 6
E-Recruiting

Things You'll Learn in this Section

41	Using the Recruiter's Work Center Dashboard to Manage Your Requisitions and Applications	122
42	Conducting Efficient Background Checks	124
43	Managing Your Recruiting Administration Activities with the Recruiting Administrator Role	126
44	Managing Performance Management Functions and Reporting via One Transaction	130

SAP E-Recruiting will help your company accelerate and optimize the entire staffing process, from planning through attracting, hiring, and retaining employees. The breadth of functions, including electronic screening, filtering, sorting, ranking, and workflows allow you to automate the flow of information and processes and promotes company-wide collaboration. This section of tips will help developers, business analysts, system administrators, and functional power-users in HR and IT with streamlining their staffing processes in SAP ERP HCM.

Tip 41: Using the Recruiter's Work Center Dashboard to Manage Your Requisitions and Applications

The recruiting work center dashboard is an effective and efficient tool to manage, monitor, and complete requisition and application processing.

You and your recruiting team can use the Work Center Dashboard to better manage and track the status of staffing activities, such as requisition and application processing for internal and external candidates, candidate searches, background checks, and communication. You can view key performance indicators (KPIs) to understand where in the workflow you or your recruiters need to take action and to navigate directly to the specific task or activity for completion.

The dashboard also lets you personalize the view of your query results. You can determine which columns appear and in what order.

The following is a list of standard delivered queries to help you complete your tasks and activities more efficiently:

- My New Applications
- New Team Applications
- My Planned Activities
- My Planned Correspondence
- My Planned Treasury and Rsisk Management (TRM) Activities
- Talent Groups
- New Registered Candidates

Solution

To determine how the columns will appear in the dashboard for each of the queries and then personalize them, you can use the following menu path:

> PORTAL • E RECRUITING • RECRUITER

You will see the RECRUITER WORK CENTER shown in Figure 1. You can personalize this screen to review statuses and manage your requisitions, activities, and postings, and create internal or external applications manually.

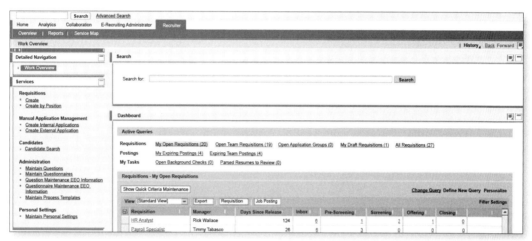

⌃ *Figure 1* Work Overview — Displays the Work Center for Recruiters Page

You can personalize the dashboard by removing unnecessary queries and keeping those that you use regularly. You can customize the sequence that the queries appear, and the columns each query contains. To customize, click on the PERSONALIZE button in the right-most corner of the screen, as shown in Figure 2.

⌃ *Figure 2* Active Queries

Click on PERSONALIZE to select the queries you want to see on your dashboard. This will help you effectively manage your requisitions and applications. ■

Tip 42 Conducting Efficient Background Checks

You can use the E-Recruiting background check functionality to verify candidate data and monitor the status of background checks.

You can use the standard functionality in SAP ERP Enhancement Pack 4 to provide enhancements for background checks and verification of candidate data. This functionality reduces the time and effort needed for you to process candidates faster and shorten the overall recruiting cycle.

During your recruiting process, you can easily and automatically initiate background checks for one or more candidates simultaneously. Although the system will not let you submit duplicate background checks, you can track the status of background checks or vendor results on the dashboard.

Vendors can access the SAP E-Recruiting system directly to provide status results. When completed, the vendor can post the results for review via a linked Website.

 Solution

To use the background check functionality, you need to have SAP ERP Enhancement Package 3 or 4, and have a background check service provider. You can initiate background check orders for multiple candidates simultaneously.

You can also initiate background check orders where the background check vendors do not need to respond immediately, but could process it and get back to you in a specified time frame.

You can also see status updates from vendors. Your vendors can update an order's status in SAP E-Recruiting themselves, without recruiters requesting an update.

You can initiate and monitor background checks in SAP E-Recruiting whenever it's convenient, because background checks can be submitted in bulk to vendors at any time.

You don't have to worry about duplicate background checks — the system prevents the submission of duplicate background check orders.

Once you've confirmed that the background check is done, use the following menu path:

> PORTAL • E-RECRUITING • DASHBOARD • MY TASKS

This powerful tool helps your recruiters increase their productivity and efficiency, and helps them complete background checks for your new hires and prehires. You can use the standard delivered interface for background-checking vendors' software to let you automate the background-check process for new employees. SAP certification helps ensure that the interface between SAP software and the external vendors' products functions smoothly. You can create a new activity for a background check request or you can monitor and track statuses, as shown in Figure 1.

⌃ *Figure 1* Dashboard

From here, click on OPEN BACKGROUND CHECKS to monitor the status of your background check requests. You can use this business function to make the process of recruiting and hiring suitable applicants more efficient and make it much easier to work with SAP E-Recruiting.

Tip 43: Managing Your Recruiting Administration Activities with the Recruiting Administrator Role

You can manage and administer your recruiting processes using the Recruiting Administrator role through a user-friendly interface in the Portal.

A recruiter is responsible for filling vacant positions and performs all tasks in the recruitment process. There are a lot of activities that a recruiter is responsible for, and instead of going to multiple places in SAP ERP HCM (which can be confusing), you can now create and release requisition tasks, search for candidates, assign candidates to requisitions, process applications, create job postings, release job postings, and much more, via the Portal.

You can manage and administer your recruiting processes using the Recruiting Administrator role through a user-friendly interface in the Portal. Your recruiting administrator can use the Recruiting Administrator role in SAP ERP HCM to complete their tasks. The administrator can use this service to support the recruitment process in your company and identify the most suitable candidates for vacant positions. You can use the Recruiting Administrator role to access all of the required information that an SAP E-Recruiting administrator needs. So, let's get started.

 Solution

You can use the Recruiting Administrator role to provide administrative support for recruiters that are involved in the recruitment process.

With Business Package 1.41, your recruiting administrator can access all of the functions and services necessary to do their work as quickly and efficiently as possible. Your recruiting administrator will be able to support user management and central system administration. Also, your recruiters can carry out transaction data management and define personal settings.

This business package provides the recruiting administrator with functions for managing data, whereas the business package for the recruiter supports recruiters in their recruitment tasks. To manage your recruiting process using the Recruiting Administrator role, the recruiting work center in the Portal contains a personal worklist for the administrator that includes a list of all requisitions that need to be deleted or reactivated, from which the administrator can maintain users, application groups, talent groups, agencies, support teams, companies, and branches; and delete external candidates, check audit trails, maintain deleted registrations for external candidates, and maintain retention periods for requisitions. The requisitions to be deleted are displayed in the content area. Additional iViews are available for the recruiting administrator on the left-hand side of the navigation panel. Some iViews can't be accessed directly via the worksets in the Recruiting Administrator role; instead, they are accessed from other iViews via object-based navigation (OBN). The iViews are:

- Data Overview
- Candidate Profile
- Requisition to Be Deleted

The Technical name of the role is:

```
com.sap.pct.erp.erecadmin.14.administration and the Technical name of
the Portal Workset is com.sap.pct.erp.erecadmin.work_overview
```

However, you need to make sure the baseline configuration for E-Recruiting and the Portal is set up to support this functionality. In addition, you can use the authorization object P_RCF_ACT (Activities in SAP E Recruiting) to add, create, change, and delete all activities in all processes for the administrator. You use the authorization object P_RCF_ACT to determine the type of activity access for a user. An activity in SAP E-Recruiting is therefore identified through the assigned process and through the activity type.

Tip 43 Managing Your Recruiting Administration Activities with the Recruiting Administrator Role

The following activity access types can be stored using the authorization field ACTVT (Activity):

- Add or Create
- Change
- Delete

You can use the authorization object P_RCF_WL to determine the worklists that a user can access in the dashboard. The user has access to all worklists that are stored in the field RCF_WL_ID (Identifier of Worklist) for the user.

First, you need to make sure you have the Recruiting Administrator role SAP_RCF_BUSINESS_ADMINISTRATOR assigned in your portal roles. You can confirm this via the following menu path:

> PORTAL • RECRUITING ADMINISTRATOR

This is the traditional path, but the menu path could vary with your company's Portal design. If it's different, you can contact your Portal administrator for the menu path applicable to your company's Portal. As shown in Figures 1 through 4, you can carry out requisition activities, such as creating a requisition.

The manager can execute the recruiting activities and create requisitions, as shown in Figure 1. Select an employee and click on CREATE REQUISITIONS, which brings you to the form shown in Figure 2.

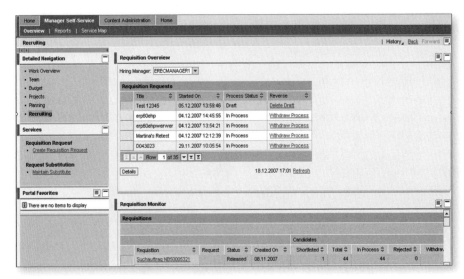

▲ *Figure 1 Manages Self-Service — Recruiting*

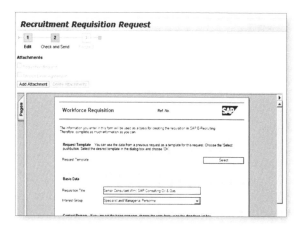

» **Figure 2**
Recruitment Requisition Request

Next, if you enter the requisition details, you get the screen shown in Figure 3. This is where you can enter the request information.

» **Figure 3**
Recruitment Requisition Request

Finally, you get confirmation that the requisition creation is finished, and the system provides you with a confirmation number, as shown in Figure 4.

» **Figure 4**
Recruitment Requisition Request

Tip 44 Managing Performance Management Functions and Reporting via One Transaction

You can use Transaction PHAP_ADMIN_PA to execute tasks related to administering and managing the appraisals process.

As an administrator for performance management activities, you may encounter locked appraisal records or be asked to prepare appraisal documents for employees or managers, change existing appraisal documents, or complete activities for managers on leave. These are many ways to do these activities in SAP ERP HCM, however, they can be very time-consuming and inefficient. Fortunately, Transaction PHAP_ADMIN_PA can perform the following activities in one easy-to-use screen:

- Prepare appraisal documents
- Find and unlock any locked appraisal documents
- Check Customizing settings
- Display existing enhancements and add any additional enhancements and relevant implementations
- Reset the status of appraisal documents
- Perform follow-up processing
- Perform further administrative functions

✓ Solution

System administrators need to report on the status of appraisals in progress (i.e., how many are in planning, completed, in preparation, or in process. You might also need to change or update an appraisal document in progress). For example, you could add or change objectives on an appraisal, or initiate a new appraisal document for an employee using Transaction PHAP_ADMIN_PA. Once you enter this transaction code, you'll see the screen shown in Figure 1. You can enter data in the selection screen per your requirements and click Execute.

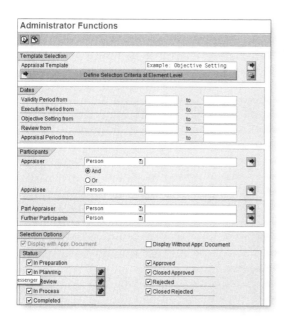

« Figure 1
Administrator Functions

Employees often get locked out of the system while working on an appraisal document and then need you to unlock it. You can also download an appraisal to work on it offline, or download the report to Excel. As an administrator, you can also reset the status or terminate the workflow.

To address appraisals for multiple employees, use the selection criteria shown in Figure 1, and click Execute. The report displays results based on your selection criteria and you can continue the administrative activities as shown in Figure 2.

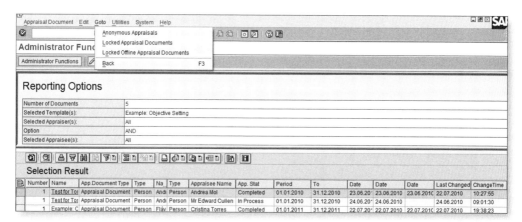

≈ Figure 2 Administrative Functions — Lock, Unlock Functionality

Part 7

Performance Management

Things You'll Learn in this Section

45	Evaluating Appraisal Results, Creating Ranking Lists, and Comparing Appraisal Documents	134
46	Changing Your Appraisal Document	138
47	Changing the Customizing Settings for Your Appraisals	142
48	Controlling Access to Training Courses in the SAP Learning Solution	144
49	Managing Your Backend Objective Setting and Appraisal Process	146

Performance management includes the support to create, plan, implement, and report on objective settings and appraisals. The appraisal systems component can be used to evaluate members of your organization in a planned, formalized, and standardized manner. Personnel appraisals are used to obtain information on the characteristics, behavioral traits, and performance of members of your organization, and form the basis for planning and making decisions that apply both to individuals and organizations. This section of tips will help the developers, business analysts, system administrators, and functional power-users in HR and IT with performance management processes and data administration in SAP ERP HCM.

Tip 45: Evaluating Appraisal Results, Creating Ranking Lists, and Comparing Appraisal Documents

You can use Transaction PHAP_SEARCH_PA to perform evaluations, compare appraisal results, and run reports for tracking purposes.

In most companies, employee performance is a direct input to ongoing compensation management decisions. It impacts merit and stock foculs, as well as bonus awards and promotions. Given this dependency, it's important to manage your performance appraisal processes carefully. Frequently, the HR organization is heavily involved in supporting the performance management process and providing support to the business as they complete appraisal related activities.

The larger a company becomes, the more difficult it is to manage successfully. The question quickly becomes how do you conduct, monitor, track, report, and analyze appraisal activity in an increasingly coordinated, timely, and efficient manner.

 Solution

You can use Transaction PHAP_SERCH_PA lets you perform the following activities:

- Create ranking lists of employee appraisal documents sorted by final results.
- Print or export employee appraisal documents to Microsoft Excel for comparison.
- Perform analyses on appraisers or appraisees.

- Compare appraisal documents for multiple employees.
- Determine total values of appraisals.
- Determine average values of appraisals.

As shown in Figure 1, you can use the steps in this solution to display the required evaluation report.

1. Call Transaction PHAP_SEARCH_PA.
2. Choose the underlying appraisal template.
3. Enter the remaining search criteria to specify your search (i.e., dates, participants, and status).
4. Click Execute. You will see the results displayed in Figure 2.

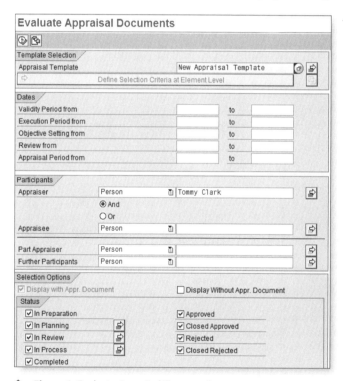

⌃ Figure 1 Evaluate Appraisal Document

Tip 45 Evaluating Appraisal Results, Creating Ranking Lists, and Comparing Appraisal Documents

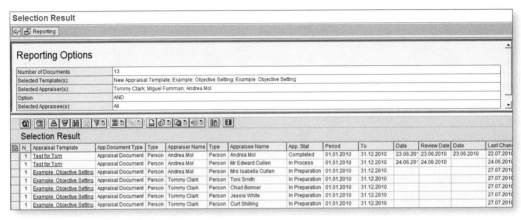

▲ *Figure 2 Reporting Options*

The system displays the evaluation/report you require. As shown in Figure 3, the output can be displayed, printed, exported to Excel, analyzed to compare appraisal documents or you can display a RANKING LIST.

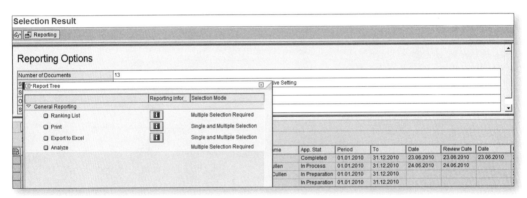

▲ *Figure 3 Reporting Options*

It's important to remember the following points regarding output:

- **Ranking:** The standard values defaults to sorting in descending order. You can only create a ranking list for appraisal documents if they have a status of Completed, Closed, or Approved.
- **Printing or Exporting to Excel:** You'll only be able to download appraisal documents that use the same appraisal template. You cannot use this function for dynamic appraisals.
- **Analyzing:** The output displays all of the results for an appraiser and all his appraisals, along with the status of the appraisals, period of the appraisal, and additional details.

Tip 46: Changing Your Appraisal Document

You can use Transaction PHAP_CHANGE_PA to make changes to objectives, body data, or header data on your performance appraisal forms.

Periodically, you may need to change the an appraisal while it is in progress. For example, you can change an appraisal document to add or delete objectives. In addition, there may be organizational changes required, such as moving an employee to a new manager or cost center. This means the new manager or supervisor has to continue or complete the appraisal cycle. The organizational changes may also require changes to the validity period for a particular objective change.

These types of edits will require you to change the header data in the appraisal document as needed. You can change the header data in the appraisal document and also change all related data regardless of the appraisal phase. You must, however, have activated the BAdI implementation. You can use Transaction PHAP_CHANGE_PA to access the appraisal document to make the necessary changes. You need to use the Change Header Data button to change the header data or the CHANGE BODY DATA button to change the body data of the actual document.

The changes made are automatically updated in the appraisal columns portion of the appraisal document. Using this functionality, you can change the following data:

- Appraiser
- Part appraiser
- Validity period of appraisal document

It's important to remember, however, that you can't change the status of the appraisal document. You can only make the changes if the appraisal is not completed and you have the right authorizations.

Solution

You can use Transaction PHAP_CHANGE_PA to change an appraisal document. This transaction lets you add new objectives, or delete existing ones, for appraisal documents that are already in process or in part process. You can only change an appraisal document if it doesn't have one of the following statuses: Completed, Closed Approved, or Closed Rejected. To use this transaction, you should have the proper authorizations, and use the following steps to select the required appraisal document and make changes to it.

1. Call Transaction PHAP_CHANGE_PA.
2. Select the APPRAISAL TEMPLATE.
3. Enter data to specify the search criteria.
4. Click Execute.

Using the preceding steps, you can select the underlying appraisal template and enter the data for an appraiser or appraisee in the selection screen, as shown in Figure 1.

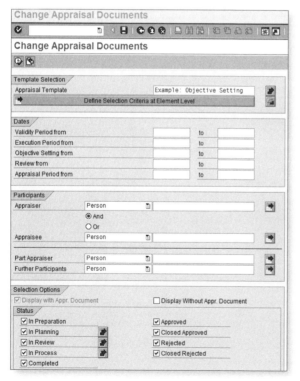

« *Figure 1*
Change Appraisal Document

Tip 46   Changing Your Appraisal Document

In Figure 1, the APPRAISAL DOCUMENT selected is APPRAISAL TEMPLATE, and the appraisers are STEVE MAGUIRE, TOMMY CLARK and MIGUEL FURNMAN (see Figure 2).

Click Execute, and you will come to the output screen shown in Figure 2, which displays the list of appraisals for the selected appraiser.

The changes made are automatically updated in the appraisal columns of the appraisal document.

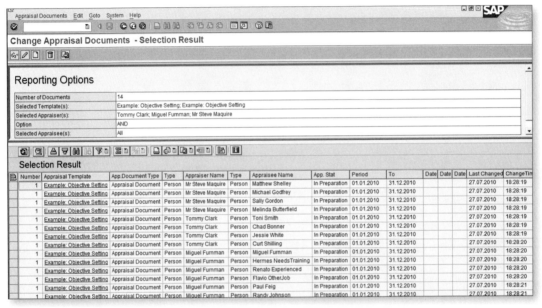

⌃ *Figure 2 Change Appraisal Document — Selection Result*

You can select the appraisal you want to change and click on the Change icon. You will see the screen shown in Figure 3.

Click on the DEFINE OBJECTIVES button at the top, and you'll see the screen shown in Figure 4.

Performance Management **Part 7**

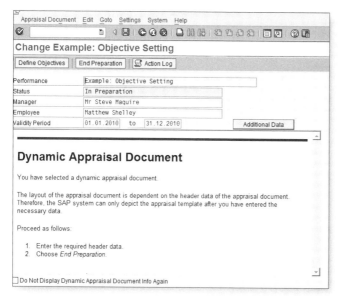

⌃ *Figure 3 Change Example — Objective Setting*

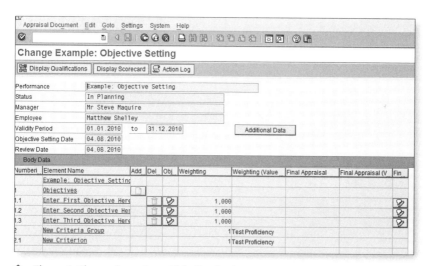

⌃ *Figure 4 Change Example — Objective Setting*

Tip 47: Changing the Customizing Settings for Your Appraisals

You can use Customizing settings to change performance appraisals, assessments, and 360° and workflow.

In the Performance Management module, you can create and process your appraisals. Employees, managers, and administrators can perform planning, reviews, and appraisal delivery. You can also run various reports to track and evaluate the process.

You may need to use the Customizing settings to make changes to performance appraisals or assessments, 360° appraisals, workflow events, or authorizations. You can create reuseable appraisal templates in the Appraisal Catalog and use them to create general appraisal documents centrally or appraisal documents for specific individuals. You can define objective setting agreements manually or automatically by integrating with other SAP components in the appraisal documents. You can also execute follow-up processing for appraisal documents and transfer information to other application components automatically. For example, you can transfer qualifications to Personnel Development or valuation results to Compensation Management for processing into rate-based salary increases or bonuses.

Solution

You can alter Customizing settings to define business criteria for appraisal processes, or maintain column layouts, roles, workflow events, and maintain authorized persons for workflow using the basic settings. Your appraisal template forms the basis for appraisal documents. You need to assign your appraisal template a category in the hierarchical structure of the appraisal catalog. Categories can include multiple templates for different appraisal types. For example, you can create different templates for employees in management positions and salaried employees. This lets you specify different objective criteria and performance evaluation processes for each of these employee groups.

You can set up appraisal templates under the description, layout, columns, columns access, value descriptions, roles, element access, processing, and status flow tabs.

- Columns tab
- Columns Access tab
- Value Descriptions tab
- Roles tab
- Element Access tab
- Processing tab
- Status Flow tab

> HUMAN RESOURCES • PERSONNEL MANAGEMENT • PERSONNEL DEVELOPMENT • SETTINGS • CURRENT SETTINGS • EDIT APPRAISAL CATALOGUE

Left-click the valuation class field and press the F1 key to display the help dialog box shown in Figure 1.

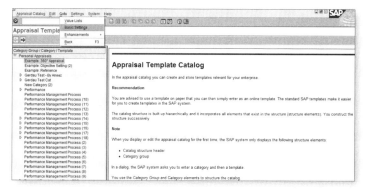

« *Figure 1*
Appraisal Template

Implementation Guide (IMG) configuration and customization can be very confusing if not done regularly. You can easily maintain appraisal customizations and update appraisal settings as needed. As shown in Figure 2, you can maintain various values via basic settings.

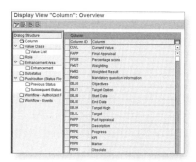

« *Figure 2*
Change View — Column: Overview

Tip 48: Controlling Access to Training Courses in the SAP Learning Solution

The SAP Learning Solution will simplify the management and control of learning activities in your organization.

You can edit your employee's access to training courses offered via the SAP Learning Solution quite easily. E-learning simplifies challenges that employers and employees are faced with in traditional classroom training activities. Classroom training ties up time and resources, takes employees away from their day-to-day tasks, and is expensive. Through the SAP Learning Solution, employees can access course content at their own pace through their desktops/laptops at work or at home.

The SAP Learning Solution offers a number of features that can ease the learning management function within an organization. You can control access to a particular course, including specifying the number of times a participant may access the content of an online course. This can be specified in Infotype 5008 and stored for the course type. The standard SAP system logs the current number of accesses per learner in the booking document PAD614. You can change the access counter per learner and increase or decrease the value. You can also set the value to zero for unlimited access.

Solution

The SAP Learning Solution lets you change the following details per participation in training management:

- **Learning object:** Specifies how many learning objects of a course have already been completed by a participant.
- **Learning objectives:** Specifies how many learning objectives of a course have already been attained by a participant. A course could consist of 15 learn-

ing objects with 12 learning objectives assigned. Of these, the learner has so far completed ten objects and attained ten objectives. Learning objects and learning objectives determine when a web-based training (WBT) is considered passed.

- **Accesses:** Specifies how often course content may be called in the Learning Portal.

You can make changes to learning objects, objectives, and accesses via Transaction LSO_ETCHANGE. As an administrator, you can enter the time specifications for a course. You can make different specifications in Infotype 5008 for an employee for a course. A course can always be canceled, regardless of whether it already started or not. You can access Infotype 5008 via Transaction PA30 or by using the following menu path to control access to Learning courses:

SAP LEARNING SOLUTION • TOOLS • DATABASES • RESET ACCESS COUNTER

The preceding transaction or menu path will bring you to the screen shown in Figure 1, where you can edit participation in time-independent courses.

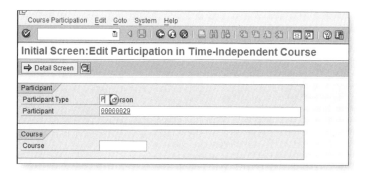

▲ *Figure 1* Edit Participation in Time-Independent Course

You can enter the values under the PARTICIPANT and COURSE fields, and select the DETAIL SCREEN. Here, you can also change entries under LEARNING PROGRESS FOR LEARNING OBJECTS, LEARNING OBJECTIVES, and ACCESSES. In the dialog box, INITIAL ACCESS: EDIT PARTICIPATION IN TIME-INDEPENDENT COURSE appears. You can enter the values you require under PARTICIPANT and COURSE by choosing the detail screen. You will see the Edit Participation in Time-Independent Course dialog box appear. You can change the entries under LEARNING PROGRESS FOR LEARNING OBJECTS AND LEARNING OBJECTIVES. Once you've made your entries be sure to save them.

Tip 49 Managing Your Backend Objective Setting and Appraisal Process

You can easily execute and manage your backend objective setting and appraisal process without having to remember menu paths or cumbersome screen navigation by using the transaction codes.

You can implement your enterprise strategy for employee appraisal and performance management using the objective setting process. You can establish a process integrating your company's overall objectives to those of each organizational unit, department, or team. You can set up task planning in each department with your employees and monitor the completion of these tasks in the review and appraisal process. You can also integrate this process with performance-related compensation adjustments for employees.

You can design and set up an appraisal process in an appraisal catalog using a category and template defined for the category. You can create appraisal documents using the category as well. The following are the standard delivered templates:

- Individual Appraisal
- Multisource Appraisal
- Part Appraisal

However, it is often very difficult to remember the menu paths and the transaction codes, especially when these transaction codes are not used frequently, so you have to keep referring to your training manuals and notes. To make your life easier and simplify access for appraisal process administration, this solution provides a complete list of the most important transaction codes.

Executing these appraisals requires the use of several transactions in the backend SAP and on Employee Self-Services (ESS)/Manager Self-Services (MSS). To simplify access to the backend, the table in the solution lists the most required and useful transactions for the objective setting and appraisals process.

It's important to note that you'll likely need specific authorizations to access the following transaction codes and you must have customized your backend to execute these transactions.

Solution

To execute the required step in your process administration in the SAP backend, use the following transactions:

Transaction	Executable Action
PHAP_CATALOG_PA with integrated transactions OOHAP_BASIC OOHAP_VALUE_TYPE	You can call the appraisal catalog. You can make basic settings for the appraisal template. You can make settings for categories.
PHAP_PREPARE_PA	You can create several appraisal documents. You can also prepare several appraisal documents using organizational units.
PHAP_CREATE_PA	You can create an individual appraisal document.
PHAP_CHANGE_PA	You can change appraisal documents. You can also change or update previously created appraisal documents, for example, you can add or delete objectives.
PHAP_SEARCH_PA	You can run evaluations or reports (only display the function). Also, you can create ranking lists, export documents to Microsoft Excel, and use analysis tools.
PHAP_ADMIN_PA	You can execute administrator functions. You can also find and unlock any locked appraisal documents, check Customizing settings, display an overview of existing Business Add-Ins (BAdIs) and relevant implementations, reset statuses, perform post processing, prepare templates and documents, and execute further administrative functions.
PHAP_START_BSP	You can generate Internet addresses.

Part 8

Compensation Management

Things You'll Learn in this Section

50	Designing a Salary Increase Program on a Single Worksheet	150
51	Adding or Changing the Layout of Compensation Planning Worksheets	154
52	Tracking and Monitoring Compensation Planning Changes	156
53	Notifying the Planning Manager to Start Compensation Planning	158
54	Managing and Monitoring your Compensation Budget Reconciliation through the Planning Cycle	160
55	Deleting Sensitive Compensation Planning History Data from the Test Environment	162
56	Controlling Exceptions on Eligibility for Compensation Plans	164
57	Mass Updating Basic Pay Based on Changes during Compensation Planning and Review for Changes	166
58	Managing Compensation Administration Activities via Compensation Specialist Roles in the Portal	168
59	Customizing the MSS ECM Screen Layout to Hide Unnecessary Columns	172
60	Adjusting Your Compensation Process Records	174
61	Renaming Column Headers in the MSS–ECM Compensation Planning Worksheet	176

Enterprise Compensation Management (ECM) is a comprehensive solution, combining backend and web-based technologies, that helps you plan remuneration policies effectively and keep costs under control, motivate and retain your employees, create and allocate budgets, and handle job pricing with the salary survey tool. This section of tips will help developers, business analysts, system administrators, and functional power-users in HR and IT with compensation management processes and data administration in SAP ERP.

Tip 50: Designing a Salary Increase Program on a Single Worksheet

You can design your compensation management program to work on a single ECM worksheet. This allows your managers to execute awards for their organizational unit with multiple plans tied to a single budget using the same worksheet.

Most users know how to create multiple plans as part of the annual compensation management cycle using separate ECM worksheets. What you may not know, however, is that this can be done with a single ECM worksheet using one budget. For example, you can set up merit, promotion, and special adjustment programs in a single ECM MSS Worksheet using multiple tabs. All three plans can be tied to the same budget and review, provided they all update Infotype 0008 — Basic Pay. You can also tie bonus plans together if they update Infotype 0015 after the activation of the awards.

Moving from tab to tab within the same worksheet is much easier and less time-consuming than saving work, exiting a worksheet, opening a new worksheet, saving work, and so on. When using one multi-tabbed worksheet tied to a single budget, managers can review and edit the three plans together. Planning is quicker and more effective because you can easily see the changes to budget distribution for an organizational unit on the same worksheet.

 Solution

To display all compensation plans in the same worksheet in different tabs and tie the plans to the same budget, follow the steps outlined here. In this example, the compensation review is called Comp Planning 2009. This review has three plans included in it: Focal Merit, Focal Promotion, and Focal Special Adjustment. All three plans are tied to the same budget.

So, to get to the compensation review, use the following menu path:

> IMG • PERSONNEL MANAGEMENT • ENTERPRISE COMPENSATION MANAGEMENT • COMPENSATION ADMINISTRATION • COMPENSATION PLANS AND REVIEWS • DEFINE COMPENSATION REVIEWS

Figure 1 begins the process of defining the COMPENSATION REVIEW.

« Figure 1
Change View —
Compensation Review:
Overview

In the next step (Figure 2), click on DEFINE COMPENSATION REVIEW. This screen is used to assign all of the plans to be used in our Comp Planning 2009 example. You'll see the MERIT PLAN, PROMOTION PLAN, and SPECIAL ADJUSTMENT plans assigned to Review M009 Compensation Planning 2009.

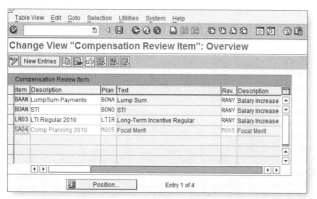

« Figure 2
Change View —
Compensation Review Item:
Overview

In Figures 3 and 4, the same budget is assigned to the MERIT and PROMOTION plans.

Once you've created the review and assigned the plans and budget, you can review Figures 5, 6, and 7 to see the three plans assigned to the same budget (M001) and displayed in three separate tabs on the same worksheet.

Tip 50   Designing a Salary Increase Program on a Single Worksheet

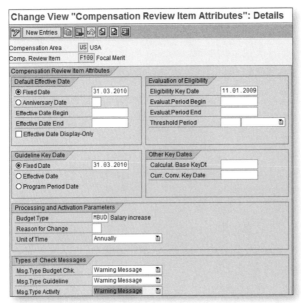

« *Figure 3*
Change View — Compensation Review Item Attributes: Details

« *Figure 4*
Change View — Compensation Review Item Attributes: Details

Figure 5 displays COMP PLANNING 2009 in the COMPENSATION REVIEW ITEM selection screen. As you can see, the same budget (M001) is assigned to MERIT PLAN, PROMO PLAN, and SPECIAL ADJUSTMENT. Also, the three plans are on the same worksheet in tabs next to each other.

This lets the manager view and conduct compensation planning efficiently by being able to move between tabs and see the changes to the budget distribution for his organizational unit on the worksheet.

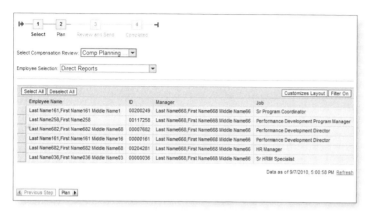

« Figure 5
Compensation Planning — Select

Figure 6 displays three tabs related to one budget structure displayed on the worksheet.

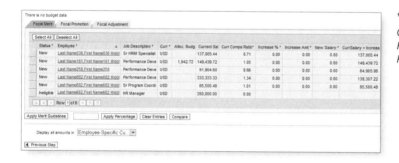

« Figure 6
Compensation Planning — Plan

Figure 7 displays COMP PLANNING 2009 in the COMPENSATION REVIEW selection screen.

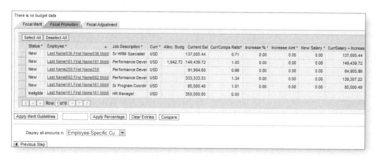

« Figure 7
Compensation Planning — Review

Tip 51: Adding or Changing the Layout of Compensation Planning Worksheets

The standard delivered column layout of the compensation planning worksheet doesn't always meet the needs of managers. You can easily modify the layout and rearrange these columns in your ECM MSS Worksheet.

Your Enterprise Compensation Management (ECM) planning worksheet has columns that display values for managers to view or input changes for their employees. Managers can view information such as salary, pay grade, organizational unit, job, position information, and so on, in the columns displayed on the worksheet. They can also enter changes to the amount in percentage or amount fields. It's not uncommon that the standard delivered columns layout isn't ideal for your business needs, so you need to change the order of the columns. For example, you may want to move certain columns, such as Performance Rating and Comp Ratio ahead of others. This can significantly reduce the amount of scrolling required to see the most relevant information.

Solution

You can add new columns to display additional information that managers need to make more informed compensation planning decisions. You can add columns to your ECM worksheet via standard customizations under the Object and Data Provider (OADP) configuration.

After making changes, you can log on to the ECM MSS Compensation Planning Worksheet to see the changes. You will see that the columns have been rearranged in the worksheet. This will let the manager see the columns in an order that makes compensation planning decisions easier.

You can rearrange the layout of columns in the planning worksheet via the following menu path:

> IMG • Integration with Other SAP.com Components • Business Packages/Functional Packages • Manager Self Service (my SAP ERP) • Data Provider • Define Column Groups

Click on DEFINE COLUMN GROUP and you will see the screen shown in Figure 1.

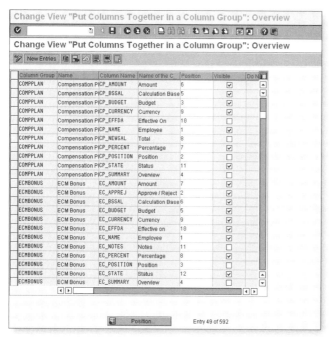

⇞ *Figure 1* Change View Puts Columns Together in a Column Group — Overview

Scroll down to select your column group for your COMPENSATION PLANNING WORKSHEET. The column position ordering determines the position of a given column on the worksheet from left to right. You can rearrange the order by changing the numbering and clicking Save.

You can see the changes in your worksheet by logging on to the ECM MSS Compensation Planning Worksheet. Select the COLUMN GROUP and then use POSITION to rearrange the orders. The columns will appear in numerical order on the worksheet starting from left to right. To configure a column so that it is always displayed (and not hidden by user options on the planning screen), select the VISIBLE checkbox. You can hide a particular column by checking the DO NOT DISPLAY checkbox. Be sure to save your entries. ■

Tip 52 Tracking and Monitoring Compensation Planning Changes

Using the standard delivered reports in SAP ERP HCM allows you to monitor all changes made to compensation planning data in Infotype 0759.

Display Compensation Planning, a standard delivered report in SAP ERP HCM, provides detailed information on the following:

- Monitoring the progress of the compensation planning cycle
- Reviewing awards made to employees
- Auditing awards made by managers so that they comply with company guidelines and policies
- Tracking changes made to Infotype 0759 by managers, including new, modified, or deleted records
- Monitoring the user IDs that make the changes

As you know, Infotype 0759 is generated or updated when a manager saves a suggested compensation award in Manager Self-Service (MSS) for a salary increase, bonus award, or long-term incentive (LTI) award. You can also maintain it manually to handle individual cases or by means of the Create Compensation Process Records report. You will see, depending on the compensation category for a salary increase, a bonus, or an LTI, either the amount/percentage (salary/bonus) or number fields (awards) displayed.

So, using this report will let managers and administrators display the changes made to Infotype 0759.

 Solution

To execute the Display Compensation Planning report, you need to specify the employees, compensation plan(s), and review(s) to track using the selection criteria. You can further specify the selection criteria by selecting the start and end dates, or by entering the name of the person who last changed the corresponding data.

You can also narrow the report output greatly by selecting the DISPLAY CURRENT STATUS ONLY checkbox. When this checkbox is selected, the report output will only display the current status of the selected planning records for that review. If this checkbox is not selected, the entire history of the selected records is displayed. By using this report, you can see the changes made to Infotype 0759 by managers and administrators. You can now easily monitor the progress of your compensation cycle example, download it to a spreadsheet, and review the awards made to the employees. You can also conduct an awards audit and discuss with managers any award that is outside company policy.

To get to the Display Compensation Planning report, use the following menu path:

> HUMAN RESOURCES • PERSONNEL MANAGEMENT • COMPENSATION MANAGEMENT • ENTERPRISE COMPENSATION MANAGEMENT • COMPENSATION PLANNING • MONITORING • DISPLAY COMP. PLANNING CHANGES TO ACCESS THIS REPORT

Enter the details in SELECTION CRITERIA and click Execute. You will see the output as shown in Figure 1.

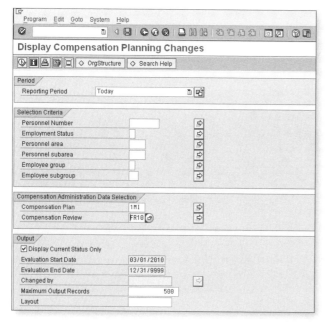

« Figure 1
Display Compensation Planning Changes

Tip 53 Notifying the Planning Manager to Start Compensation Planning

RHECM_NOTIFY_MANAGERS is the report in SAP ERP HCM that distributes notifications to initiate planning for organizational units or employees for the new compensation cycle.

It is critical to notify all planning managers to start the compensation planning cycle once the budget structures have been created and released. Notifications can be sent by executing the standard delivered report RHECM_NOTIFY_MANAGERS. You can also add customized messages to the notification emails.

The report triggers a workflow template (WS04000025) that sends out the notifications. The notification process history is stored in table T71ADM_PROCESS, recording that notification took place for the affected organizational units.

Notifications are only sent to planning managers that have employees eligible for review and who are directly reporting to the planning manager. It's important to remember, however, that Infotype 0105 — Communication — must exist for the subtype 'user' and has the email address of the planning manager.

 Solution

You can access the report via Transaction SE38, which you can also get to via the following menu path:

> HUMAN RESOURCES • PERSONNEL MANAGEMENT • COMPENSATION MANAGEMENT • ENTERPRISE COMPENSATION MANAGEMENT • COMPENSATION PLANNING • PREPARATION • NOTIFY MANAGERS

You can only send notifications using this report when the following conditions are fulfilled.

You should make sure the corresponding process/review you are sending the notification to is active. Also, you need to make sure the SEND NOTIFICATION checkbox is made active in the IMG customization of the corresponding compensation review.

Employees who occupy a chief position within an organizational structure will be considered a Planning Manager and will be sent the notification. In addition, the Planning Manager's Infotype 0105 must have the user ID and email address in order for the notification to be sent to the Planning Manager. Also, you can only send notifications to planning managers that other employees report to directly, provided that these employees are eligible for review.

Once you execute the report, you will see the message shown in Figure 1 conforming that the notification has been sent to the managers of the organizational unit chosen in the selection screen.

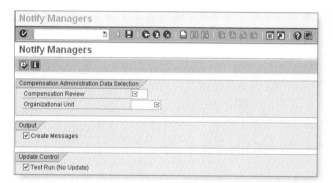

« *Figure 1*
Notify Managers

From here, you can select the COMPENSATION REVIEW from the drop-down list for which you want to notify planning managers to commence planning. Enter the ROOT ORGANIZATIONAL UNIT from the drop-down list to select all of the managers that need to be notified. You can check the TEST RUN (NO UPDATE) box to do a test run.

Tip 54 Managing and Monitoring your Compensation Budget Reconciliation through the Planning Cycle

You can review and audit the budgeted allocation amounts versus the actual spending and remaining balance based on your organizational hierarchy. This can be done while your compensation planning process progresses or when it is completed.

The compensation department is required to track the progress of budget spending during the compensation process. They are also usually required to complete an audit process after each cycle is completed.

You can easily create a report to generate details such as budgeted amount, amount awarded, and budget remaining for each unit. The report produces an output mirroring your budget structure/organizational structure. If you are in a global environment and need to distribute reports to multiple people for specific portions of the organizational structure, you can do so by running the report per organizational units.

You can run this report for both monetary budgets (bonuses, salary increases) and long-term incentive awards (LTIs).

Solution

The Monitoring of Compensation Budgets report (RHECM_BUDGET_RPT) is a standard budget monitoring report. This report displays budgeted and spent amounts for compensation plans. It provides an overview (budgeted, spent, and roll-up amounts) per organizational unit. This report can be shared with your executive team to review budget distribution and compliance by planning managers. Running this report at the start, during, and end of a cycle to monitor budget distribution is a best practice.

To get to the report, use Transaction SE38 and select RHECM BUDGET RPT.

Click on the report and enter the details as BUDGET TYPE, BUDGET PERIOD, BUDGET UNIT, and ORGANIZATION UNIT in the selection screen, as shown in Figure 1.

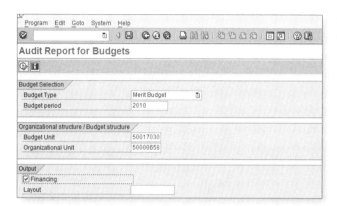

« *Figure 1*
Audit Report for Budgets

Enter the BUDGET TYPE, BUDGET PERIOD, BUDGET UNIT, and ORGANIZATION UNIT in the selection criteria and click Execute. You will see the output with details of the budgeted amount distributed by ORGANIZATIONAL UNIT, as shown in Figure 2.

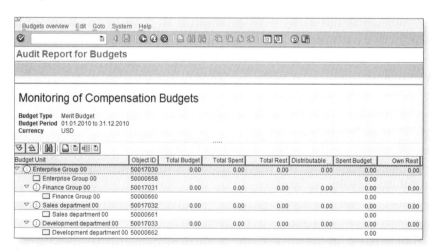

▲ *Figure 2 Monitoring of Compensation Budgets*

Tip 55: Deleting Sensitive Compensation Planning History Data from the Test Environment

You can quickly delete any sensitive compensation plan data from the test environment once the review and test have been completed.

The SAP standard delivered report RHECM_DELETE_HISTORY_DATA allows you to clean up sensitive compensation planning data from the test environment. This report deletes all planning history data for a review that has been completed. It also deletes any associated data stored in the employee history and process history tables along with the employee notes, compensation review notes, and spent amounts.

The report can only be executed after the review period for the selected review has elapsed. You can execute this report in test mode to see the data being deleted and then run it in real mode with the test box unchecked.

 Solution

Use report RHECM_DELETE_HISTORY_DATA to manage and clean up your compensation planning history data.

First, use Transaction SE38 and enter report RHECM_NOTIFY_MANAGERS in the selection screen, or use the following menu path:

> HUMAN RESOURCES • PERSONNEL MANAGEMENT • COMPENSATION MANAGEMENT • ENTERPRISE COMPENSATION MANAGEMENT • COMPENSATION PLANNING • FOLLOW-UP • DELETE COMP. • PLANNING HISTORY DATA TO ACCESS THIS REPORT

You can execute this report by specifying a completed compensation review, in which you now want to delete data from the employee and process history tables. Select the TEST RUN (NO UPDATE) checkbox (which is selected by default), as shown in Figure 1.

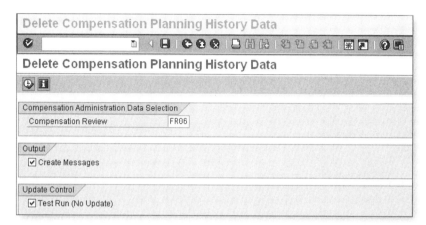

⌃ *Figure 1* Delete Compensation Planning History Data

Enter the data in the selection screen and click Execute. The report will delete compensation planning history data as described previously.

Upon execution, this report displays a summary of the data it has deleted (if executed in production mode) or would delete (if executed in test mode). The output of the report is displayed for you to review. Keep in mind that the report can only be executed after the review period for the selected review has elapsed. ■

Tip 56 Controlling Exceptions on Eligibility for Compensation Plans

You can make exceptions for employees who aren't eligible for salary increases but need to be made eligible for specific compensation plans. This can be done after the eligibility rules for compensation plans have been defined.

Using Infotype 0760 — Eligibility Override — you can control an employee's eligibility for a given compensation plan for a certain period. This infotype can control an employee's micro-eligibility by overriding the eligibility criteria defined in the customization. This helps in situations where some of your employees are not typically eligible for a special bonus program, but you've received direction from management to make an exception.

 Solution

You can create a record of Infotype 0760 and make the employee micro-eligible by entering the date on which their eligibility becomes effective in the ELIGIBILITY DATE field, as shown in Figure 1. If this field is left empty, the employee is eligible during the entire validity period of this infotype. The eligibility date can only be used when the EE IS ELIGIBLE box is checked.

If you don't maintain Infotype 0760, then the eligibility for the employee is checked based on the rules defined in Customization. This is a very effective way of handling exception cases without having to do ABAP. This infotype can also be used to make eligible employees ineligible for a particular compensation program for a certain period.

To override eligibility for exception cases, you can select the employee and Infotype 760. You can make the employee eligible or ineligible, as shown in Figures 1 and 2.

To maintain the HR master data, use the following menu path:

> HUMAN RESOURCES • PERSONNEL MANAGEMENT • ADMINISTRATION • HR MASTER DATA • MAINTAIN

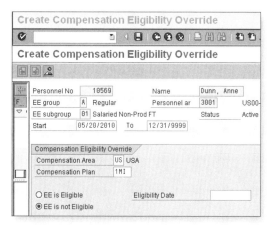

⌃ *Figure 1* Create Compensation Eligibility Override

Enter the employee number you want to override eligibility for and select Infotype 0760. Enter the COMPENSATION PLAN that you want to override eligibility on, and enter the eligibility date. This is the date that the employee becomes eligible or ineligible for the plan, as shown in Figure 2.

⌃ *Figure 2* Create Compensation Eligibility Override

Tip 57 — Mass Updating Basic Pay Based on Changes during Compensation Planning and Review for Changes

Mass updates to Infotype 0008 — Basic Pay — can be performed for all impacted employees to reflect changes to Infotype 1005 during the planned compensation activities.

It's important to update Infotype 0008 to correctly reflect changes made to Pay Grades/Pay Scales in Infotype 1005. New pay grade assignments are date-driven and delimit the old ones. The values for Pay Scale type, Pay Scale area, Pay Scale group, and Pay Scale level in Infotype 0008 are defaulted from Infotype 1005 assignments on jobs or positions.

Manual updates are cumbersome and developing a new program is expensive and time-consuming. The standard delivered report RHECM_UPD_0008_FROM_1005 in SAP ERP can be used very effectively for mass updates to Infotype 0008. This report updates Infotype 0008 with the changes to pay scale type, area, group, and level to reflect the values in Infotype 1005. If the result conflicts with the salary range, the business logic of Infotype 0008 returns an error or warning message, depending on the setting in table T710A.

 Solution

You can make mass updates to Infotype 0008 to reflect the changes you have made to Infotype 1005 automatically using report RHECM_UPD_008_FROM_1005. To get to this report, use Transaction SE38, and select RHECM UPD 008 from 105. Enter the required values in the selection screen, including the date for the basic pay change record. This will be the new effective date for changes reflected in Infotype 0008, as shown in Figure 1. You can execute this report in test mode first. You will see the output shown in Figure 2. When satisfied with the results, you can uncheck the Test Run (No Update) box and click Execute to do the real update.

Compensation Management   Part 8

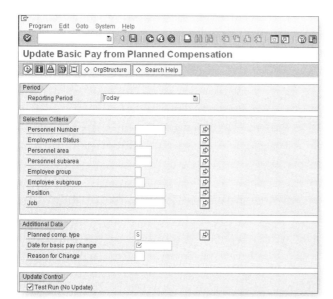

« Figure 1
Update Basic Pay from Planned Compensation

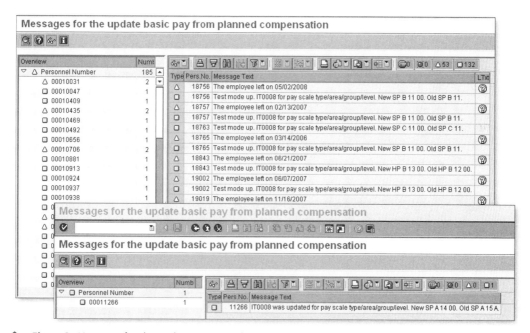

≈ Figure 2 Messages for the Update Basic Pay from Planned Compensation

The message shows Infotype 008 has been updated for pay scale type/grade changes for PERSONNEL NUMBER 11266.

167

Tip 58: Managing Compensation Administration Activities via Compensation Specialist Roles in the Portal

Your compensation specialist can use the SAP ERP HCM Compensation functionality to evaluate, develop, adapt, and promote effective company policies.

The Compensation Specialist role is tightly integrated with all of the functionality of the Enterprise Compensation Management (ECM) components. Using the standard delivered Compensation Specialist role, your compensation specialist can perform all tasks related to compensation administration using the Portal's intuitive and user-friendly interface and iViews instead of using R3 on the backend. This will greatly improve the user experience and efficiency when completing activities such as salary increases or short- and long-term incentives.

Managing these activities is straightforward, if you know what to do, which brings us to the following solution.

Solution

The business package in SAP ERP HCM enhancement package 4 is aimed at compensation specialists. It supports the tasks a compensation specialist typically performs, such as:

- Preparing job descriptions and conducting individual job evaluations and reviews.
- Managing participation in salary surveys to monitor competitive market trends to evaluate, compare, develop, and adjust pay structures (grades, ranges, etc.).

- Create compensation budget structures, allocate budgets, and reassign budgets within the organizational structure.
- Execute compensation reports using the Compensation Specialist role in Manager Self-Service (MSS).
- Consult and advise employees, managers, and HR staff on compensation-related issues.
- Communicate the compensation policy to management and employees.
- Support strategic projects by aligning project objectives and the corresponding compensation/long-term incentive plans.

The SAP technical name of the Compensation Specialist role is com.sap.pct. compspecialist. You need to make sure the IT team assigns this role to the compensation administrator so that they can perform these activities.

To get to the COMPENSATION SPECIALIST screen, use the following menu path:

PORTAL • COMPENSATION SPECIALIST

As a compensation specialist, you can choose the activity you want to do from the screen shown in Figure 1.

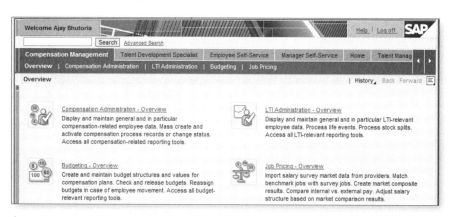

↥ *Figure 1* Compensation Management

From here, you can perform administration tasks regarding salary increases, as shown in Figure 2.

Tip 58 Managing Compensation Administration Activities via Compensation Specialist Roles in the Portal

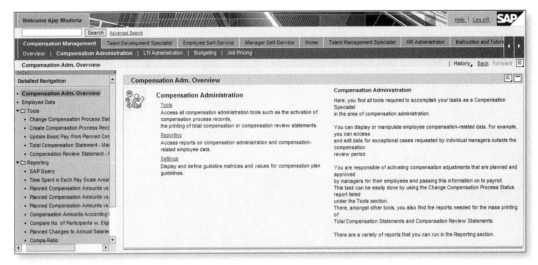

▲ *Figure 2 Compensation Administration Overview*

You can perform BUDGETING activities via the screen shown in Figure 3.

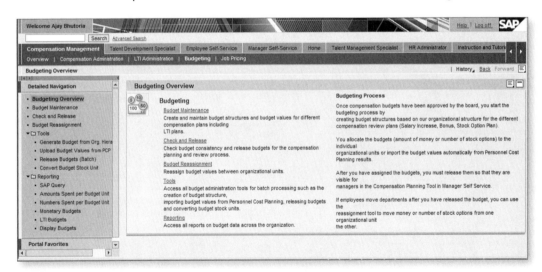

▲ *Figure 3 Budgeting Overview*

Finally, you can carry out activities related to JOB PRICING via the screen shown in Figure 4.

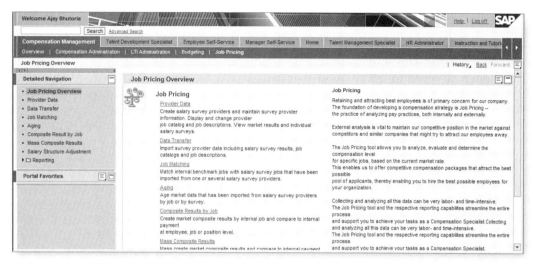

⌃ *Figure 4* Job Pricing Overview

As you can see, the compensation specialist role in SAP ERP HCM Enhancement Pack 4 leverages the portals' intuitive interface to access all the standard delivered ECM functionality. Your compensation team can perform all their administrative duties. Activities such as configuration, employee data maintenance, managing budget structures, market analysis, coordinating jobs and pay structures, reporting, and executing compensation programs through MSS will be much easier. ◼

Tip 59 Customizing the MSS ECM Screen Layout to Hide Unnecessary Columns

You can customize your view of the SAP Compensation MSS ECM Planning Worksheet by selectively displaying only those columns that you want to see.

The MSS ECM Planning Worksheet screen often includes more information than you need about an employee's job, such as position, organizational unit, new salary, old salary, old compensation ratio, new comp ratio, notes, and so on. If you're a planning manager using the worksheet, you have to scroll back and forth to see all of the employee data, or to see a particular column at either end of the worksheet. This is not an ideal user experience and often leads to negative user feedback.

 Solution

Managers can choose which columns they would like to display on the worksheet from a pool of available columns in the MSS ECM Planning Worksheet. A manager can use the default setting on the standard screen as shown in Figure 1.

Or, you can click on the CUSTOMIZE LAYOUT button, which brings you to a list of all of the columns in the worksheet. From there, you can select/deselect the columns you want to see on the screen. The settings will be available for reuse the next time you log in to the MSS-ECM Planning Worksheet.

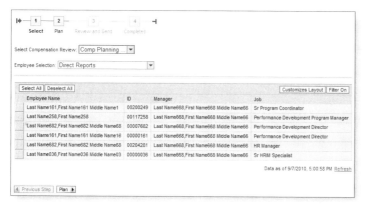

⯅ Figure 1 Compensation Planning

To customize the layout and display of the worksheet, you can select, deselect, and change the order of the columns in the worksheet by first navigating the following menu path:

> MANAGER SELF SERVICE • ECM • COMPENSATION PLANNING

Click on the CUSTOMIZE LAYOUT button in the upper right-hand corner. You'll see a list of all of the columns. Select the columns you want to have included in your worksheet by checking the selection box and click Save. Refresh your screen or log back in again, and you'll only see the columns you have selected displayed in your worksheet, as shown in Figure 2.

⯅ Figure 2 Compensation Planning

This screen displays the columns you have selected. Those columns not selected are not displayed on the worksheet. ■

Tip 60 Adjusting Your Compensation Process Records

Let's say your organization has decided to preload Infotype 0759 — Compensation Awards — for all employees during a salary increase with percentage increases based on set guidelines and your company has also decided to make a mass change to all employee records in Infotype 0759 after the planning has been completed. You can do mass updates to Infotype 0759 records using a standard program.

Often, during a salary increase cycle or short-term increase cycles, it is necessary to mass update employee Infotype 0759 records. You may need to do mass updates to Infotype 0759 to update all compensation planning awards submitted by planning managers during or after the planning cycle, or to apply standard guideline-based percentage increases for all employee records in Infotype 0759. You can also selectively delete Infotype 0759 records for a group of employees.

Doing these activities manually would be time-consuming and cumbersome. Or you may have to develop a custom program to manage the above requirement, which could be expensive. SAP ERP delivers a new report in enhancement pack 4 that lets you perform mass changes to, or deletions of, records in Infotype 0759. You can also perform status changes on Infotype 0759 records or create new records for employees who don't have an Infotype 0759 record for specific plans using this report. It's best to run this report in the Test Run mode first to confirm the changes, and then run it in actual mode by deselecting the Test Run box.

Solution

The SAP system allows you to mass update Infotype 0759 records. You can adjust percent increases for all records or you can create new records by applying guidelines set up in your customizations. You can also delete records. To start, use Transaction SE38 and enter report RHECM_CREATE_COMP PROCESS in the selection screen.

In addition to the standard time-dependent and organizational criteria, enter the COMPENSATION PLAN and COMPENSATION REVIEW that you want to make adjustments to in the Infotype 0759 records. You can adjust the percentage by entering the new amount, bringing it to the minimum to replace the current compensation amount with the minimum amount of the salary range the employee belongs to as of the effective date, and provided that the current amount is lower (note that this option is limited to compensation plans defined as salary adjustments), or apply guidelines by clicking the radio button. If you want to delete existing records, you can select the DELETE RECORDS radio button, as shown in Figure 1. Click Execute, which will update/adjust Infotype 0759 per your selection criteria.

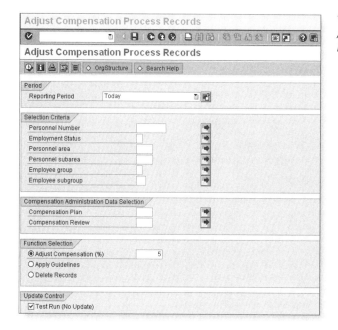

« *Figure 1*
Adjust Compensation Process Records

The output of the report is a list of the compensation records that have been generated successfully for the selected employees, containing either the adjustment amount and the currency, or the number of awards. If an error occurs, the personnel number is skipped and an error is displayed.

You should note, however, that this report is intended for mass processing. Execution should be done in the background via PROGRAM • EXECUTE • BACKGROUND. It is also strongly recommended that you perform a test run to identify and correct any errors before you update the database.

Tip 61: Renaming Column Headers in the MSS–ECM Compensation Planning Worksheet

Renaming the SAP standard MSS ECM Worksheet column headers to align with your company's terminology can be done easily.

It is not uncommon for companies to use terminology that is different from what is delivered by SAP ERP HCM, as standard ECM worksheet column headers. For example, you might want to change the column Grade/Level to "Grade" only, or, you might want to rename the header Job Description to "Job Title." You can easily rename these column headers without it becoming an expensive and time-consuming custom development project. Changes like these can be completed quickly and easily using the standard customizations in SAP ERP HCM, as outlined in the following solution. For example, the following are some of the standard delivered columns in the ECM worksheet.

- EC_AMOUNT (Amount)
- EC_APPRAISAL (Appraisal)
- EC_APPREJ (Approve/Reject)
- EC_BSSAL (Base Salary)
- EC_BUDGET (Budget)
- EC_COMMISS (Commissions)
- EC_COMPRATIO (Compa Ratio)
- CP_CURRENCY (Currency)
- EC_EFFDA (Effective On)

You can change the text of any of the columns and rename it per your company's commonly used verbiage to make it easier for a manager to understand. For example, you could change Base salary to Basic Pay. So, let's get started.

Solution

The Object and Data Provider (OADP) enables you to arrange data flexibly in ECM. For each individual plan category (salary, bonus, long-term incentive (LTI) plan), you can store your own settings for the Compensation Planning and Compensation Approval iViews and columns. You can also store your own settings for each compensation plan. You can rename the column headers per your organization's needs and terminology using the following steps. Once you make the changes and save them, you can log back in to the MSS ECM Compensation Planning Worksheet to review the changes. You need to make the changes in your Development environment to test them and then transport the configuration to Production when done. This makes it easier for you to rename a column per your company's needs and use your company-specific lingo.

To start, use the following menu path:

> IMG • INTEGRATION WITH OTHER SAP.COM COMPONENTS • BUSINESS PACKAGES/FUNCTIONAL PACKAGES • MANAGER SELF SERVICE (MY SAP ERP) • DATA PROVIDER • DEFINE COLUMN GROUPS

Select the column you want to rename, enter the new name, and click Save, as shown in Figure 1. Under the column heading, you can change the text of the column headers and click Save. You can see the changes to the column header text by logging back into the ECM Compensation Planning Worksheet. As you log in to the MSS ECM Worksheet, you will see the columns with the new text.

« *Figure 1*
Change View — Column Definition

Part 9

Career Succession and Planning

Things You'll Learn in this Section

62	Comparing Talent Profiles Using the Compare Functionality	180
63	Using Succession Planning to Organize Your Processes	182
64	Designing Your Job Architecture for Efficient Succession Planning	184

Career succession planning includes the Talent Management/Development and Succession Planning functions. In a dynamic business climate it is very important for an organization to have a career succession planning process in place, especially for its key positions. If a key position becomes vacant, it needs to be filled quickly and with the right person. You can use the Succession Planning function to ensure that key positions are identified and potential successors are assigned. You can use the talent management/development process to develop and foster talent in your enterprise. You can hire personnel, further educate and develop your talents, and align your employees with enterprise goals. This section of tips will help developers, business analysts, system administrators, and functional power-users in HR and IT with career succession and planning processes and data management in SAP ERP HCM in a more efficient and effective manner.

Tip 62: Comparing Talent Profiles Using the Compare Functionality

You can compare multiple talent profiles and view side-by-side comparisons of results by managers and talent management specialists.

Talent management specialists can use the compare function to select and display multiple talent profiles for a side-by-side comparison of different criteria. For example, you could compare or contrast talent with similar performance results.

 Solution

There are a number of different options available for using the compare functionality within Talent Management, including:

- Using the Compare option that is available in the CALIBRATION GRID, BUSINESS CARD, or LIST VIEWS.
- Dragging and dropping talent photos onto the COMPARE TALENT screen.
- Selecting multiple talents using the COMPARE button in the TALENT SEARCH IVIEW.
- Selecting multiple talents in the TALENT INFORMATION IVIEW.

To use this functionality, you'll need to make sure that the customization is done in IMG under TALENT DEVELOPMENT • SETTINGS.

To do the required customization in the IMG, use the following menu path:

> BASIC SETTINGS • ADJUSTING THE USER INTERFACES • CONFIGURATIONS FOR DATA RETRIEVAL • CREATE CONFIGURATION WITH FIELD GROUPS • CREATE A CONFIGURATION

Under ASSIGN USER INTERFACE CONFIGURATION, assign it to the TALENT_SHORT_PROFILE_SDIEBYSID parameter.

As you can see in Figure 1, you can edit the configuration.

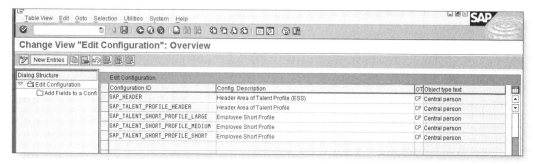

↥ *Figure 1* Change View "Edit Configuration" — Overview

You can compare talents in Manager Self-Service (MSS) in the Talent Search iView and display the results as shown Figure 2.

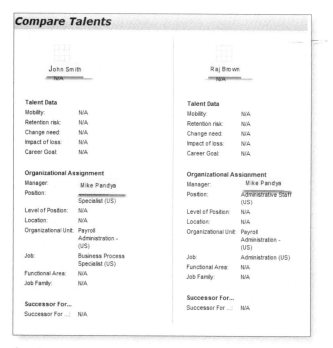

↥ *Figure 2* Compare Talent Display and Compare Talents in MSS

Tip 63: Using Succession Planning to Organize Your Processes

You can use the Succession Planning functionality to organize a succession planning process for key positions.

In a dynamic business climate, it's important for an organization to have a succession plan in place for its key positions. If a key position becomes vacant, it needs to be filled quickly with the right person. You can use the Succession Planning functionality in SAP ERP HCM to ensure that key positions are identified and potential successors are assigned. The following information can be defined for possible successors:

- **Nomination Status:** Nominated or Approved. Once approved, the individual becomes an active participant in the succession planning process.
- **Reason for Assignment:** Provides a reason for the assignment and identifies which talent management specialist made the assignment.
- **Ranking:** Provides a value that can be used to differentiate potential successors relative to each other or a ranking value that the successor is to assume when occupying the newly vacated position.
- **Readiness:** Provides an assessment of the successor's readiness for a new position and a time frame the employee is available to move into a new position.

So, let's get started.

Solution

To define succession planning for positions, you can use one of the following three standard delivered relationships in Organizational Management (OM):

- **Is Successor Of/Has Successor (740)** — between the employee (OBJECT CP) and the position (OBJECT TYPE S) for assigning successors. Using this relationship, you can classify employees as potentially suitable for jobs in a job family and create a successor pool.

- **Has Potential For/Is Potential Of (744)** — between the employee (OBJECT TYPE CP) and the job family (OBJECT TYPE JF) for assigning an employee to the job family.
- **Has Talent For/Comprises Talent (743)** — between the employee (OBJECT TYPE CP) and the talent group (OBJECT TYPE TB) for assigning an employee to the talent group.

To get to these options, use the following menu path:

> PORTAL • MANAGER SELF SERVICE • TEAM

You can do succession planning in Manager Self-Service (MSS) and review the employee information, as shown in Figures 1 and 2.

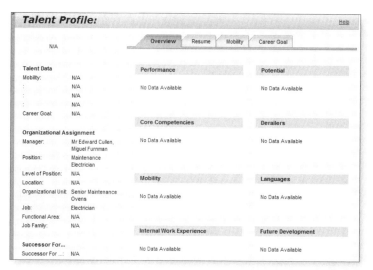

« Figure 1
Talent Profile

« Figure 2
Assessment

Tip 64: Designing Your Job Architecture for Efficient Succession Planning

You can define your succession plan for your organization with a well-defined job architecture.

Often, the Career Succession Planning module doesn't work accurately because you don't have your Job Architecture defined clearly. Due to the lack of a well-defined job catalog and functional areas, you can't define clear succession plans. It is very important that you have a well-planned, clearly defined, and organized job architecture to support succession planning. The key elements of a job architecture include a catalog with functional areas, job families, jobs, and positions. In succession planning, there are several objects in Job Architecture that you can define and edit, such as Functional area (object type FN), Job family (object type JF), Job (object type C), and Position (object type S).

Solution

Defining the correct hierarchical relationships between the objects is critical (usually a tree structure). Some of the key relationships that should be used are:

- Functional area comprises job families (relationship 450)
- Job family comprises job(s) (relationship 450)
- Job comprises position(s) (relationship 007)

You can also assign competencies (qualifications, object type Q) to the functional areas, job families, jobs, and positions. The competencies get assigned automatically to the entire lower level structure. So if you have assigned certain qualifications to the functional area, it will automatically get passed on to the job families and from there to the jobs and finally to positions.

To edit the job architecture, you can use the Nakisa 2.0 (and above) visual graphical interface or Transaction HRTMC_PPOC. You can also use the following menu path, which will bring you to the screen shown in Figure 1:

> HUMAN RESOURCES • PERSONNEL MANAGEMENT • PERSONNEL DEVELOPMENT • SETTINGS • CURRENT SETTINGS • EDIT CAREERS

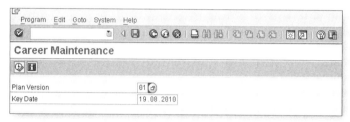

˄ *Figure 1* Career Maintenance

You can represent hierarchical relationships, such as the organizational structure, job architecture, or an indirect reporting structure (i.e., a tree structure). You can also specify the organizational unit each talent management specialist in your enterprise is responsible for managing (Figure 2).

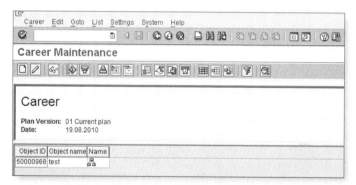

˄ *Figure 2* Career

Your accurate definition of your Job Families and relationships will support creating accurate and efficient management of careers in career succession planning. In Figure 2, you can run reports based on various criteria, as discussed, and get the output on careers. You can analyze the employee career data and maintain it easily. ■

Part 10

Employee Self-Service and Manager Self-Service

Things You'll Learn in this Section

65	Displaying Table Contents for Master Data Fields	188
66	Control Settings for Subtype Display on ESS	190
67	Personalizing Your Workflow Task List Display Page	192
68	Control the Visibility of Personal Information Fields on Employee Self-Service (ESS) Screens	196
69	Multiple Ways You Can Search for Employees in Manager Self-Service (MSS)	198
70	Launching Manager's Desk Top Reports from the Launch Pad in MSS	202
71	Setting the Approval Working Time in MSS Using the Collective Approval Screen	204
72	Controlling Absence and Attendance Types Displayed in Multiple iViews in ESS	206
73	Using Guided Procedures to Streamline the User Experience for Benefits Enrollment and Life and Work Events in ESS	208
74	Controlling Personnel Information Infotypes for Employees	212
75	Customizing Your System Messages on Employee Self-Service	214

ESS and MSS provide advantages such as a central point of entry; secure role-based access to applications, services, and information; and personalization. ESS lets all employees create, display, and change employee-relevant data themselves. MSS provides managers with applications and services they need. By giving your employees and managers access to their own data and processes, you simplify and standardize HR activities and free up your HR department for more value-added tasks. This section of tips will help developers, business analysts, system administrators, and functional power-users in HR and IT with ESS and MSS processes and data management in SAP ERP HCM in a more efficient and effective manner.

Tip 65: Displaying Table Contents for Master Data Fields

You can easily hide an iView or a specific section of a page in MSS so that you can display only the pages you want to see.

Most organizations have at least thought about customizing the content in the ESS or MSS pages in their Portal to better meet their needs. There should be an easy way to hide an iView or a section of a page that is being displayed. For example, in the Team Workset in MSS, in the General Information section, you might not want to display the Employee Photo, Company Properties, and Related Activities sections. In the following solution, you'll learn how to do just that.

Solution

As shown in Figure 1, the standard page for General Information shows these sections by default. You can easily hide these sections by going to PORTAL • CONTENT ADMINISTRATION using the following steps. You can review your MSS pages and identify sections to edit property values for, or do not want to display. If you change your mind later, you can use these same steps to edit property values further, or add the hidden sections back in to the display. It's important to remember, however, that you'll need Portal Administrator authorization to do this activity.

First, use the following menu path:

> PORTAL • CONTENT ADMINISTRATION

To hide or display a section on a page in MSS, you need to log in to the Portal and go to the CONTENT ADMINISTRATION page, as shown in Figure 2.

Employee Self-Service and Manager Self-Service   **Part 10**

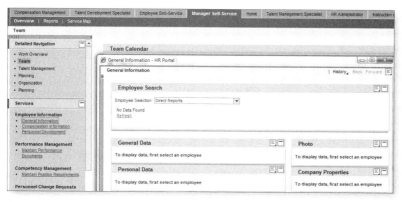

▲ **Figure 1** MSS — Team: General Information

▲ **Figure 2** Content Administration

Select your organization's Portal Catalog. Under MANAGER SELF SERVICE, select the page you want to display or hide. You can also edit properties such as renaming a page by changing the name value in the PROPERTY EDITOR, as you can see in Figure 2. After completing your changes, click Save. When you log back in you will see the changes you made, as shown in Figure 3.

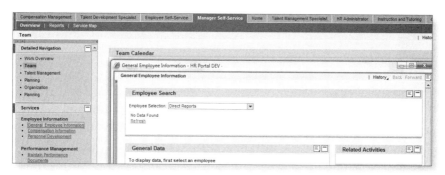

▲ **Figure 3** MSS — Team

As you can see, the page name was changed to GENERAL EMPLOYEE INFORMATION and the section PHOTO and COMPANY PROPERTIES sections are hidden.

189

Tip 66 Control Settings for Subtype Display on ESS

You can control the settings on ESS to allow employees to edit certain infotypes or create future-dated records.

It's easy to customize the Personal Information section in ESS by individual country. You can control which subtypes are active for infotypes such as Address (IT0006), Bank Information (IT0009), and Dependents (IT0021), and are displayed. You can also set the following indicators for each infotype and subtype to show which items your employees are able to create and edit:

- **Allow Future Data Records:** Allows your employees to create future data records with start dates in the future. If the indicator is not set, the system will not display future dated records.
- **"New" pushbutton Always Available:** Allows your employees to create new data records. The system will display the "New" button on the application overview page.
- **Valid Data Record Required:** Shows that a valid data record will always exist for the employee for as long as that employee is active.

✓ Solution 1

In the standard ESS, employees are not permitted to create data records with a future valid-from date for every infotype, but they can for infotypes such as Addresses (006). You can also allow certain sub types to be displayed and edited on ESS. For example, with Infotype 0006 you can allow the subtypes PERMANENT and EMERGENCY ADDRESS to be displayed and edited. Complete the steps below to enable users to add an item to a subtype or change an existing item:

1. Check the active subtypes for each infotype for the relevant country.
2. To add a new subtype, choose NEW ITEM.
3. To change interface behavior, set or delete the relevant indicator for the infotype and subtype.
4. To de-activate an active subtype, delete the corresponding item from the table.
5. Save your entries.

PERSONNEL MANAGEMENT • EMPLOYEE SELF-SERVICE • SERVICE SPECIFIC SETTINGS
• OWN DATA • DETERMINE ACTIVE SUB TYPES AND MAKE ACTIVE SETTINGS

Click on the IMG step and use the drop-down menu to select the COUNTRY to which you are making changes. Select the INFOTYPE for which you want to add/drop a subtype or make changes to the INDICATOR and update the RECORDS, as shown in Figures 1 and 2.

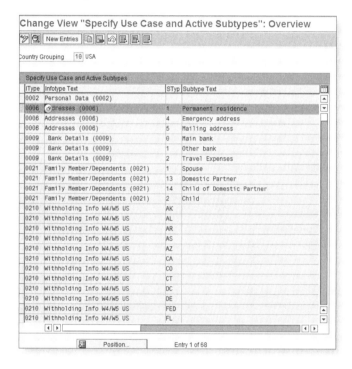

« Figure 1
Task List

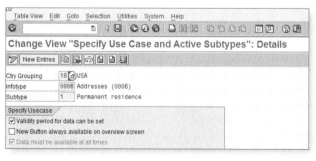

« Figure 2
Task List — Personalize Task

Tip 67 Personalizing Your Workflow Task List Display Page

You can personalize your Workflow Task List display page in a variety of ways to improve usability and increase your productivity.

You can personalize your Workflow Task List in the Portal to make it easier and faster for you to review and assess work items that require immediate attention. For example, you can:

- Select the attributes you want displayed, including From, Escalated, Escalated By, Item Type, Status, and so on, and the order in which you want them displayed.
- Define the number of items you want displayed on each page. You can also define the default setting for sorting preference.
- Define data properties, such as the Page Refresh Rate. This will automatically refresh the page after five minutes to display new work items and delete old ones.
- Set up a system warning to alert you prior of an action's due date.

✓ Solution

You can personalize the standard Task List page in SAP ERP HCM to make it easier and faster for you to process your pending workflow items. To start, use the following menu path:

> PORTAL • LOGIN INTO PORTAL (ESS/MSS) • TASK LIST

Left-click on the PERSONALIZE VIEW icon, as shown in Figure 1.

Employee Self-Service and Manager Self-Service **Part 10**

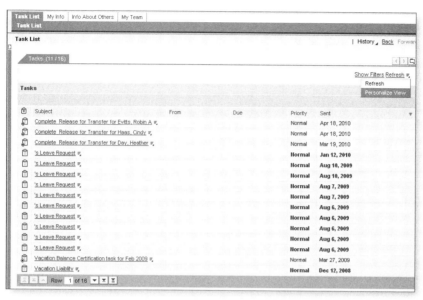

⚠ *Figure 1* Task List

As you can see in Figure 2, the screen shows the different sections for personalization. By clicking on the PERSONALIZE VIEW icon in Figure 1, you get to Figure 2. This is where you can personalize ATTRIBUTES, SORTING PROPERTIES, DATA PROPERTIES, and PAGE DISPLAY.

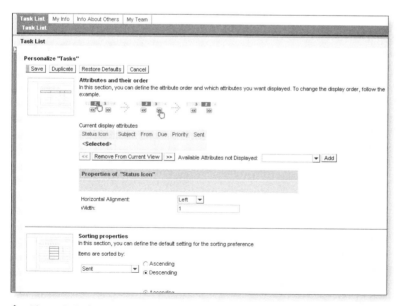

⚠ *Figure 2* Task List — Personalize Tasks

193

Tip 67 *Personalizing Your Workflow Task List Display Page*

You can add an attribute (column) to display on task list by clicking the Add icon, or you can remove an attribute from the layout by clicking on REMOVE FROM CURRENT VIEW, as shown in Figure 3. You can also change the order in which you want to display attributes.

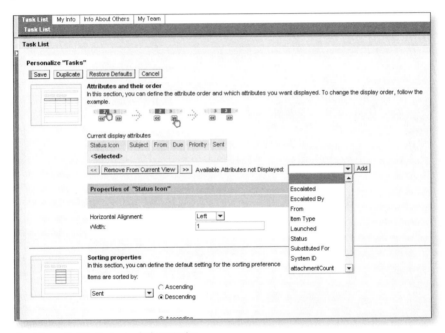

▲ **Figure 3** *Attributes and Their Order*

Finally, you can personalize the items to be displayed per page, or the page refresh rate, by selecting the values from the drop-down lists (see Figure 4). The refresh timing will refresh your task list with any new items or remove any processed items, which keeps your list clean and minimizes potential confusion.

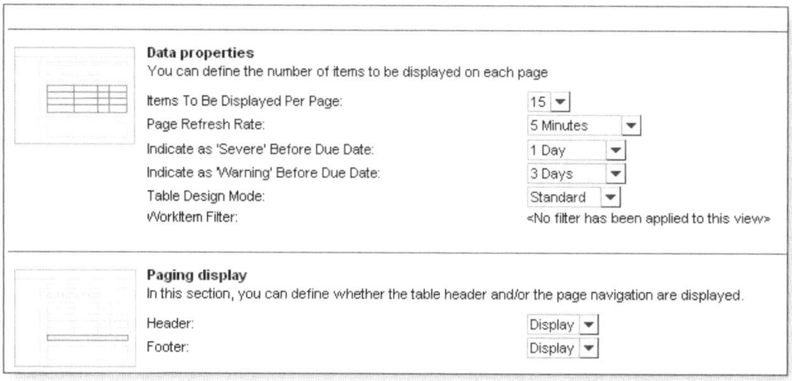

↑ *Figure 4* Data Properties and Paging Display in Personalize Tasks

You can display the workflow tasks in a list. You can sort the entries in the different columns of the list. For example, you can display all workflow tasks which are overdue together, or you can get an overview of the priority and due date of the various workflow tasks. You can also define substitutes who process workflow tasks in your absence. On the details page, you can execute, reserve, confirm, and forward a workflow task.

Tip 68: Control the Visibility of Personal Information Fields on Employee Self-Service (ESS) Screens

You can control and make changes to fields in ESS for personal information Infotypes by making them editable.

In earlier versions of SAP ERP, making modifications to ESS, such as changing personal information infotypes to hide fields or making fields editable, required, or optional was done in the HTML templates of the ESS service in question. In ERP ECC version 5.0 and higher, you can easily maintain screen control much like the screen control done for PA20/PA30 infotypes using table V_T588M. In this case, you can use table V_T588MFPROPS through SM30/31 to control the visibility of fields on ESS screens. By changing the setting in table V_T588MFPROPS, you can make a field on an ESS screen required, hidden, or output (display) only. Through screen control, you can also remove fields from the screen or make them optional or display only.

 Solution

To control the visibility of fields in ESS from Infotypes 0002 (Personal Data) and 0006 (Address), and other personal information infotypes, you can use table V_T588MFPROPS. Enter the infotype number and hide the fields for a country-specific version.

You can use Transaction SM30, and enter table V_T588MFPROPS. You can check the boxes and make the fields required, hidden, fixed, or display only.

After you make and save the changes, you can log in to ESS and see the changes you made.

Enter the infotype number under Work area and click Enter. You will see the screen shown in Figure 1. You can scroll down to select the country version and you can make changes to the ESS screen setting for this infotype.

« Figure 1
Determine Work Entry Area

Enter the table name V_T588MFPROPS, click on MAINTAIN, and then select the infotype that you want to maintain for field control and click Enter, which will bring you to the screen shown in Figure 2.

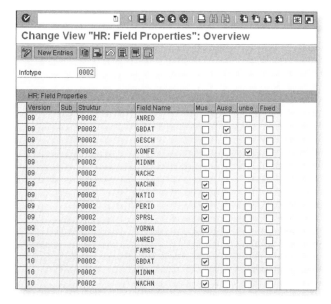

« Figure 2
Field Properties

You can choose which fields are going to be REQUIRED, HIDDEN, FIXED, or DISPLAY ONLY by checking the appropriate box. After you have made your changes, save your entries. Log in to ESS under the PERSONAL INFORMATION section and review the changes you made for screen control.

Tip 69 Multiple Ways You Can Search for Employees in Manager Self-Service (MSS)

Managers can search for employees in MSS in multiple ways using the standard delivered search functionality.

Often, managers get confused about how to search for employees in the MSS functionality. Sometimes managers need to get a list of all direct reports, or a list of all indirect reports, or a list of all employees in their organizational structure. A manager may be looking for a specific employee and searching by last name. Managers need to search for their team members in MSS to process different activities, such as giving salary increases in Enterprise Compensation Management (ECM), time approvals, processing forms, hiring, and termination, and so on. You can help managers search efficiently using the standard search capabilities as described in the following Solution.

✓ Solution

There are different views provided for a manager to conduct a search:

- **Directly subordinate employees:** Provides a list of employees reporting directly to the manager, as shown in Figure 1.
- **Employees from organizational structure:** Provides managers with a structure of his organizational units. Once he selects an organizational unit from the structure, the list of employees assigned to this organizational unit is displayed on the right side, as shown in Figure 2.

- **Employees from organizational units:** Provides the manager with a list of organizational units he is responsible for. The manager can select one or more organizational units form this list. Once he clicks on the Go button, the list of employees assigned to the selected organizational units is displayed on the screen, as shown in Figure 3. To select a second organizational unit from the list, use `CTRL` + mouse-click on the second object in the list.
- **Employee search:** Provides an additional way to find an employee. This search scenario makes sense if the manager doesn't have a lot of information about the employee he is searching for.

The search is a backend search. This means the system identifies the employees that match the search criteria in the SAP ERP system and displays the results on the front end. In the standard implementation, a manager can search by last name, first name, middle name, or personnel number. The search allows for the following:

- Enter the correct and full information in one or more of the fields (e.g., Colazzo (Last name), Francesco (First name), or 1941 (Personnel Number))
- Enter wildcard search entries (e.g., C* or C+lazzo)
  Note: The search is case sensitive. Once the manager has entered entries in the fields, he needs to press the Go button

The Employee Search iView is based on an object and a data provider. The employee search is an iView that is used for the employee, position, and organizational unit profile pages. It enables managers to select an organizational object from the list. The other iViews on the same Portal page react to this selection. This function is called Eventing.

The Employee Search iView acts as a sender whereas the other iViews on the portal page act as a receiver. Once the manager has selected an object (e.g., an employee) from the employee search, the object ID is sent to the other iViews. These iViews compare the sent ID with the current ID. If the sent ID differs from the current ID, the iView retrieves the appropriate data of the new ID from the backend system and displays it in the iView. The Employee Search is an iView that is used for the Employee, Position, and Org Unit Profile pages.

Tip 69 Multiple Ways You Can Search for Employees in Manager Self-Service (MSS)

Figure 1 shows the multiple ways to search for an employee using the drop down for EMPLOYEE SEARCHES in different iViews in MSS. The DIRECTLY SUBORDINATE EMPLOYEES view provides a list of employees reporting directly to the manager.

« **Figure 1**
Employee Search

In Figure 1, you can search an employee using his LAST NAME, FIRST NAME, PERSONNEL NUMBER, ORGANIZATIONAL UNIT, PERSONNEL AREA, and PERSONNEL SUBAREA. Based on the selected parameters, employees will be displayed in the output results. If a manager has multiple organizational units, he can select employees using organizational structures. The selection will display all the organizational units the manager has, and you can choose employees belonging to specific units or multiple organizational units.

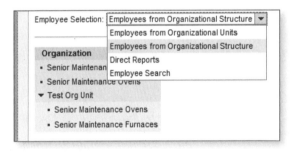

« **Figure 2**
Employee Search — Search Using Organizational Structure

200

As you can see in Figure 2, the selection shows the two organizational units the manager manages and the manager can select the organizational unit he wants to process an activity for.

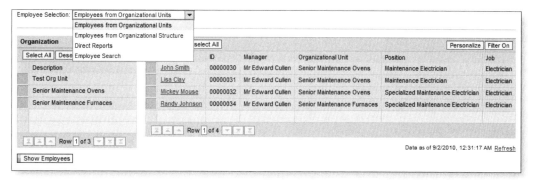

⌃ *Figure 3* Employee Search — Search Using Organizational Units

The EMPLOYEES FROM ORGANIZATIONAL UNITS selection provides the manager with a list of organizational units for which he is responsible. The manager can select one or more organizational units form this list. Once he clicks on the GO button, the list of employees assigned to the selected organizational units is displayed on the screen. To select a second organizational unit from the list, use CTRL + mouse-click on the second object in the list.

Tip 70: Launching Manager's Desk Top Reports from the Launch Pad in MSS

If you previously used MDT for your reports, you can reuse the configuration tables for MSS reporting by running the conversion report. You can easily convert your MDT reports into MSS Launch Pad report tables using the conversion report.

Many HR reports are based on entries in the Manager's Desktop tables. You need to transfer the entries to the Launch Pad tables. MDT reports can be migrated to the MSS Launch Pad by running a conversion program included in SAP ERP 6.0 and up. The Launch Pad iView displays the Manager's Desktop (MDT) reports that the manager can launch from the Launch pad. The Launch pad iView works as a launch pad to launch reports.

You can use Launch Pad framework to display a list of MDT reports that can be run by a manager. You can classify the reports into separate categories such as Benefits reports, Time reports, Payroll reports, and ECM reports. In addition, you can assign a descriptive text to each of the reports in the master list of reports. The text associated with each report can be used to give a description of the report's usage. From this list of available reports, a manager can personalize the list so that only the reports that he wants to run will be displayed in the Launch Pad.

To integrate the MDT configuration with the new Launch pad report customizing, you must run the conversion report to move the entries in the MDT tables to the Launch pad table. In addition, you must run the conversion report to update the Launch pad table each time you update your MDT customizing.

 Solution

To access this conversion report, use the following menu path:

> IMG • MANAGER'S DESKTOP • CUSTOMER ADJUSTMENT • CONVERT MDT DATA TO MSS REPORTING LAUNCH PAD

You must also configure certain parameters in the Portal Content Directory (PCD). The parameters relevant for reporting include:

- **Scenario:** Define the scenario that creates a list of available reports. In the standard delivery, the standard scenario is RPT0. The value of the scenario parameter is the MDT scenario. If you want to use the standard scenario, set the parameter scenario to RPT0.
- **Viewgroup:** Parameter viewgroup defines the Object and Data Provider (OADP) viewgroup. This viewgroup contains at least one view ID. View IDs determine the list of Organizational Management objects, such as employees and organizational units.

To get to this screen, use Transaction SPRO, and navigate the following menu path, shown in Figure 1:

> MANAGER'S DESKTOP • CUSTOMER ADJUSTMENT • CONVERT MDT DATA TO MSS REPORTING LAUNCH PAD

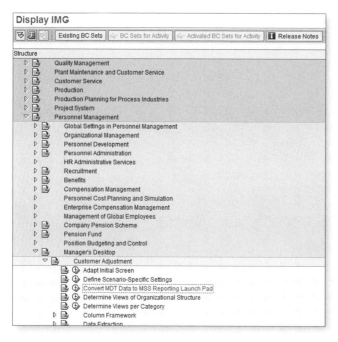

« *Figure 1*
Convert MDT Data to MSS Reporting Launch Pad

Tip 71: Setting the Approval Working Time in MSS Using the Collective Approval Screen

You can use the IMG to customize the collective and individual Cross-Application Time Sheet (CATS) approval screens in MSS, including specifying the fields and information displayed for the recorded time data.

Managers can approve employee time data using a consolidated view in the Collective Approval screen. This screen enables approval with a one-click action. Data is displayed one line item per week per employee. Managers can also view a comparison of recorded hours to target hours (work schedule) to quickly scan for overtime.

Solution

You can customize the collective and individual approval screens. You can specify which fields, and therefore, what information, is displayed for the recorded time data in the individual and collective approval views using the IMG configuration nodes via the following menu path:

> IMG • INTEGRATION WITH OTHER MYSAP.COM COMPONENTS • BUSINESS PACKAGES/FUNCTIONAL PACKAGES • MANAGER SELF SERVICE (MYSAP ERP) • WORKING TIMES • APPROVAL OF WORKING TIMES

As you can see in Figure 1, managers can perform the following actions on the COLLECTIVE APPROVAL screen:

- Approve all records for all employees
- Reject all data in one line (dropdown), with rejection reason (optional)
- Set all data in one line to resubmission (dropdown)
- Drill down to an individual approval screen (click on the SUM OF HOURS) and do an individual approval, as shown in Figure 2.

˄ **Figure 1** Approve Time by Manager — Collective Approval

˄ **Figure 2** Approve Time by Manager — Individual Approval

In addition, you can review an overview of all of the records that are rejected, set to resubmission, or approved in the REVIEW SCREEN, as shown in Figure 3. Managers can approve individual time by selecting an individual line item. As a manager, you can also reject a line item of hours or all hours. You can also define a reason for rejection. You can view all hours by clicking on the hours. You can show all approved working times for a given day or week. Once you have approved the records, you will see the REVIEW screen and you can save. You can review all of your approved hours in this screen as in Figure 3. Once you have reviewed everything, you are finished. You can also define the fields in the IMG you want to see displayed in the INDIVIDUAL APPROVAL screen and COLLECTIVE APPROVAL screen.

˄ **Figure 3** Approve Time by Manager — Review and Save

Tip 72: Controlling Absence and Attendance Types Displayed in Multiple iViews in ESS

You can use this IMG activity to create, display, and enable employee processing, and customize process workflows for absence and attendance types in ESS.

You can use this IMG activity to create and specify which absence and attendance types are displayed, and can be processed by employees, in the team calendar, overview of leave, and clock-in/clock-out corrections within ESS. You can also specify how the absences are processed and define user interface elements depending on the absence type.

✓ Solution

If you only want to display absence types in the team calendar, leave overview, or clock-in/clock-out corrections, but don't want your employees to request that type of absence, you have to select the following fields:

- EEs Not Permitted to Submit Requests
- No Changes to Leave Permitted
- No Deletion of Leave Permitted

You can also specify if you want to use the workflow function. If you want to use the workflow for leave requests, enter the required workflow template in (shown in Figure 1). You can either use standard workflow templates or your own customized copy of the workflow template 12300111. You should use workflow template 12300111 as a basis for your customized workflow templates.

To control the absence and attendance types that are available to employees in the selection criteria, use the following menu path. As you can see in Figure 1, you can use the appropriate checkboxes to control the display of leave requests and permissions to delete or submit a leave request.

> IMG • PERSONNEL MANAGEMENT • EMPLOYEE SELF SERVICE • SERVICE SPECIFIC SETTINGS • WORKING TIME • LEAVE REQUEST • PROCESSING PROCESSES • SPECIFY PROCESSING PROCESSES FOR LEAVE TYPES

From here, you can configure the Absence/Attendance Type controls.

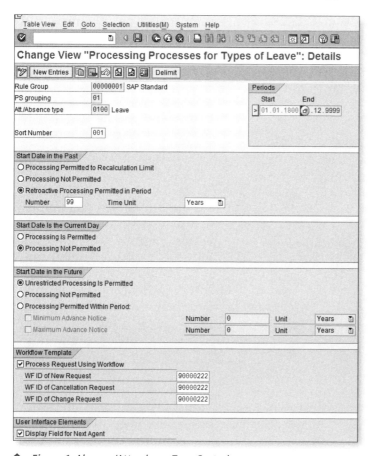

⌃ *Figure 1* Absence/Attendance Type Controls

Tip 73: Using Guided Procedures to Streamline the User Experience for Benefits Enrollment and Life and Work Events in ESS

You can use guided procedures in ESS to easily complete step-by-step processes such as enrolling in benefit programs and addressing life and work events in ESS.

Guided procedures are an automated set of steps used to guide end users through the execution of benefits-related processes that pertain to life and work events. Some examples would include the birth or adoption of a child, a change in employment status for the employee or their spouse, divorce, and marriage. Giving the end user a guide to follow helps them understand the context and complete the process more efficiently. They reduce confusion and potential for errors when completing longer or more complex procedures.

New employees are a good example to review. Users are guided through steps to complete new-hire paperwork and forms, input of personal and dependent information, and the selection of, and enrollment in, various medical, dental, vision and insurance benefit programs.

✓ Solution

To design and create guided procedures, you need access to the Portal with authorization to the GUIDED PROCEDURES tab:

1. You also need access to Design Time. This is used to create/design guided procedures. You need access to the GP Business Expert + one subrole of GP Basic User, GP Advanced User, and GP Expert User

2. You can execute and test guided procedures using Runtime. You need access to GP Runtime WC + GP User.

3. Finally, all ESS users should have access to GP User Role to use guided procedures.

As you build guided procedures, it's important to understand the concept of objects in guided procedures. The following are several important definitions:

- **Folder:** Folders are used in the guided procedure gallery to help you organize the objects that you create.
- **Process:** It initiates the guided procedure. It specifies the objective of the business. For example: My First Days.
- **Block:** Structural units that build a process. They are reusable and may contain actions, nested blocks, or processes. Items in a block can be executed sequentially, in parallel, in a loop, or the user can choose from several alternatives. For example: First Week Tasks, Second Week Tasks.
- **Actions:** These are executable units that refer to either one or two callable objects — one for execution and an optional one for display. For example: Enroll in Benefits.
- **Callable Objects:** A reusable unit that enables the execution of external applications or services. For example: HTML Page, iView, Web Dynpro, etc.

So, to get started, navigate to the following menu path:

> CURRENT PORTAL CONTENT • CONTENT PROVIDED BY SAP • PLATFORM_ADD_ONS • GUIDED PROCEDURES

Next, we need to build the guided procedure according to the following steps:

1. Create the Folder structure.
2. Create the Process.
3. Create the Block for your Process.
4. Create /Insert Action for your Block.
5. Create/Insert Callable Objects for your actions.
6. Create Callable Actions to display of your actions.
7. Define the Authorization Roles.
8. Save and Activate.

You can create a folder in the gallery, as shown in Figure 1, by clicking on the CREATE FOLDER button.

Tip 73   Using Guided Procedures to Streamline the User Experience for Benefits Enrollment and Life and Work Events in ESS

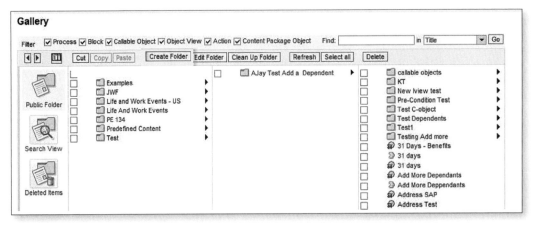

⌃ *Figure 1* Gallery

Next, you need to enter the LANGUAGE, FOLDER NAME, and DESCRIPTION, as shown in Figure 2.

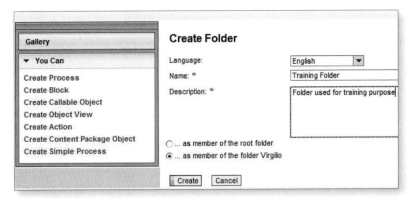

⌃ *Figure 2* Create Folder

From here, you can create the process by selecting your folder and clicking on CREATE PROCESS, as shown in Figure 3.

Create the block for processing by selecting the type of block to be used. A sequential block allows all items in the block to be processed sequentially in the order you defined (see Figure 4).

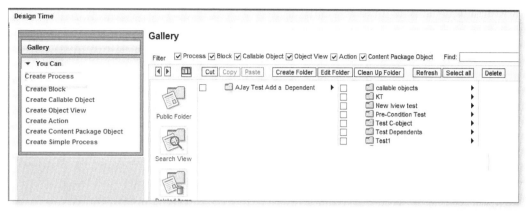

▴ *Figure 3* Gallery — Create Process

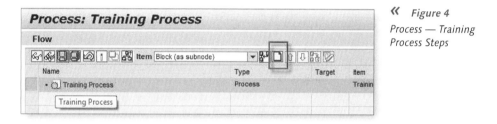

« *Figure 4*
Process — Training Process Steps

Once you activate the process, the STATUS changes to green (see Figure 5).

▴ *Figure 5* Save and Activate

You have successfully set up the guided process steps. You can design your benefits enrollment process of life event changes using the above steps. ■

Tip 74: Controlling Personnel Information Infotypes for Employees

You can control which personnel information infotypes and subtypes (by country) an employee can view or update in the Personnel Information section of ESS.

Employees can go to ESS and update personnel information infotypes such as Infotype 0002 (Personnel Data), Infotype 0006 (Address), and Infotype 0021 (Dependent Information). You may have a business need, however, to let employees view certain infotypes versus allowing them to update selected infotypes or subtypes. For example, you want to allow employees to edit data in Infotype 0006 but only for Subtype 001 — Permanent address.

You can also define the use case for each infotype or subtype.

Solution

By defining a use case, you can control which kinds of data records your employees are permitted to create. The following types are available to you: A1 to A6 and B1 to B5.

The first character indicates the validity. You can use this character to insert information about the time constraints of the data record.

- A means that data records with a certain start or end date can be created and that multiple data records can exist at the same time.
- B means that data records can also be created without a start or end date and that it is not possible to have multiple data records at the same time.

The standard setting allows the start date to be the current date or a future date. For example, on his first day of work, an employee is asked to enter his personal data in ESS. In Infotype 0002, the default validity date is from today; the start date is the data entry date and the end date is December 31, 9999. In this example, your settings have to be as follows:

Infotype	Subtype	Use Case
0002	-	B1

By using the following menu path you can create and specify active subtypes and infotypes by country and the use case for each entry, as shown in Figure 1.

IMG • PERSONNEL MANAGEMENT • EMPLOYEE SELF SERVICE • SERVICE SPECIFIC SETTINGS • OWN DATA • DETERMINE ACTIVE SUBTYPES AND MAKE SETTINGS

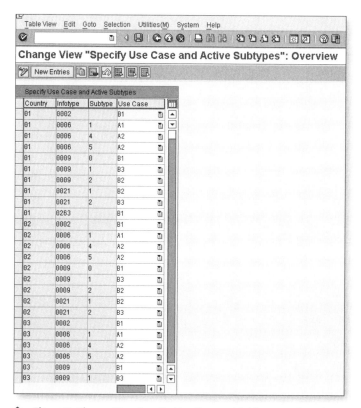

⌃ **Figure 1** Change View Specify Use Case and Subtypes — Overview

Tip 75 Customizing Your System Messages on Employee Self-Service

You can customize system-generated error messages and warning messages, or informational messages generated while executing ESS transactions.

It's not uncommon for employees to find messages generated from the SAP system to be confusing. Most times, employees don't have the knowledge or experience to understand the messages and react appropriately. You can go to the IMG activity, however, and suppress or change system messages coming from the backend system to ESS only. You'll learn how in the following solution.

✓ Solution

SAP offers the following options for modifying messages:

- Suppress an individual message or messages of an entire message class
- Suppress messages of a particular message type (e.g., if you do not want information messages to be displayed)
- Change the type of a message (e.g., change warning messages to informational messages)
- Specify alternative messages in an application area (user) and thereby determine your own message texts and message types

You can change or suppress a message, an entire message class, or for an entire application area, that is, messages from a particular application area are not to be displayed in the web application. To start, use the following menu path:

> IMG • PERSONNEL MANAGEMENT • EMPLOYEE SELF SERVICE • SERVICE SPECIFIC SETTINGS • WORKING TIME • LEAVE REQUEST • PROCESSING PROCESSES

As shown in Figures 1 and 2, you can suppress these messages by entering the name of the message class in the table and selecting the SUPPRESS MESSAGE. You can leave all other fields blank, with the exception of the one message that you don't want to be displayed. To ensure that this message is displayed, you can make entries in the APPLICATION AREA, MESSAGE TYPE, and MESSAGE fields. You leave all other fields blank. The system only displays this message when this specific message is triggered. All other messages in the application are suppressed.

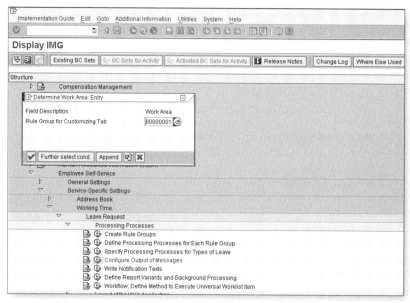

▲ Figure 1 Display IMG: Configure Output Messages

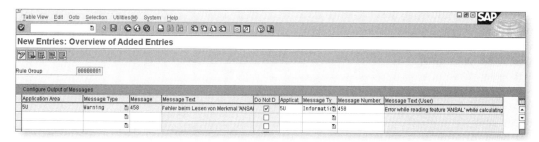

▲ Figure 2 New Entries — Overview of Added Entries

Part 11
Adobe Forms and Processes

Things You'll Learn in this Section

76	Managing the Hire-to-Terminate Employee Lifecycle Using SAP HCM Forms and Processes in MSS	218
77	HCM Forms and Process Architecture	222
78	Processing Multiple Employee's Records in Processes and Forms	226
79	Defining the Attachment Types Required for Your Form Scenario	228

The SAP Forms and Process framework offers an efficient way to manage cross-role processes involving HR master data. The highly flexible framework, using software by Adobe, allows SAP customers to build and execute their own specific processes, no matter what data, process flow, and roles are involved. This section of tips will help the developers, business analysts, system administrators, and functional power-users in HR and IT leverage the process and forms framework of SAP ERP HCM in a more efficient and effective manner.

Tip 76: Managing the Hire-to-Terminate Employee Lifecycle Using SAP HCM Forms and Processes in MSS

You can execute step-by-step processes and forms for various scenarios in the MSS and Employee Self-Service (ESS) functionalities of SAP ERP HCM.

In previous versions of SAP ERP HCM, many MSS business processes such as hiring, transfers, cost center changes, organizational reassignments, and terminations were completed using Personnel Change Requests (PCRs). These PCRs were typically inflexible and difficult to customize without investing a significant amount development time and resources. The Human Resources (HR) processes and forms framework available with SAP ERP 6.0 offers an efficient way to manage cross-role processes involving master data in SAP ERP HCM. The highly flexible framework allows SAP customers to build and execute their own specific processes, regardless of the data, process flow, and roles involved. The framework is based on three components, all of which are standard in the current version of SAP ERP:

- **HR table customizing:** Enables processes in this framework to be implemented without the need for developers to write much code
- **SAP Interactive Forms software by Adobe:** Integrates all business roles into processes through a user friendly, forms-based interface
- **SAP Business Workflow:** A workflow engine that enables improved flexibility

Adobe Forms and Processes   **Part 11**

Solution

Managers and HR administrators can start HCM forms and processes in MSS as outlined by selecting an employee, choosing a process, editing the data, and then checking and sending it.

First, use the following menu path:

> PORTAL • MANAGER SELF SERVICE • FORMS AND PROCESS

The execution involves selecting the employees the action is to be performed for. For example, if you are doing an organizational change, you would use the following steps:

1. Select Employee (Figure 1)
2. Select Process (Figure 2)
3. Edit the form (Figure 3)
4. Check and Send (Figure 4)
5. Completed (Figure 5)

The system guides you through the steps and you will get a confirmation message once the final step is completed.

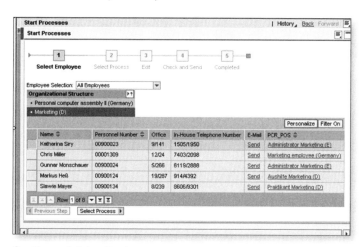

⌃   *Figure 1* Select Employee

In this step, shown in Figure 2 you select the PROCESS you want to carry out.

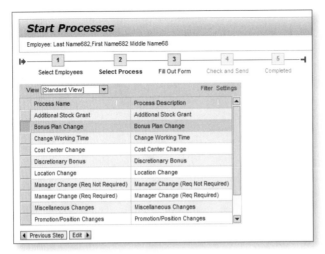

⭐ *Figure 2 Select Process*

In this step, shown in Figure 3, you enter the data into the form.

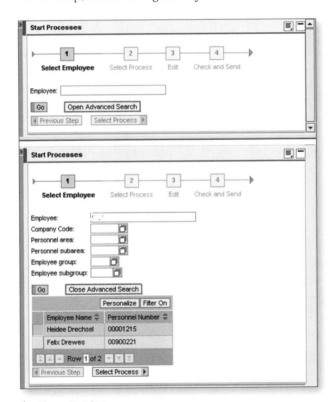

⭐ *Figure 3 Edit In*

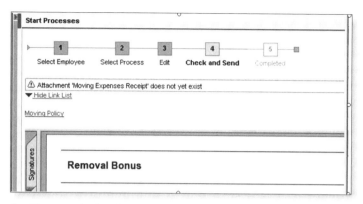

⌃ *Figure 4* Check and Send

You will see the confirmation message DATA WAS SENT.

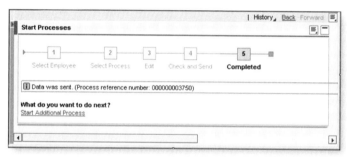

⌃ *Figure 5* Completed

Using these steps, you are able to select your employee, the process, and the data in the form. You also receive the confirmation message, as shown in Figure 5. This message confirms that the form was sent for further processing. ■

HCM Forms and Process Architecture

HR can automate a lot of regular and ongoing functions and processes using the flexible architecture of SAP Forms and Processes.

The typical HR department supports many standard functions and processes such as promotions, transfers, pay changes, leaves of absence, and terminations to name a few. These functions and processes need to be performed on a regular and ongoing basis. They often require multiple forms to be completed by multiple parties. The flexible architecture of Forms and Process allows you to automate these business processes in SAP. The processes cannot only be initiated by managers but also by HR administrators.

 Solution

You can start the creation and configuration of forms and process by using the following menu path:

> PERSONNEL MANAGEMENT • HR ADMINISTRATIVE SERVICES • CONFIGURATION OF FORMS AND PROCESS

You can take the following steps, illustrated in Figure 1:

1. Create a basic Internal Service Request (ISR) scenario
2. Create a Form scenario and define form fields
3. Configure back end services
4. Update the ISR scenario
5. Assign the Form scenario to a process
6. Define the start application
7. Configure the Form application
8. Configure the workflow

Adobe Forms and Processes   Part 11

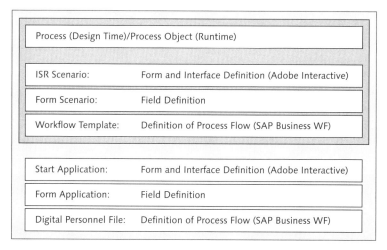

▲ *Figure 1* Creation of Forms and Process

Based on the architecture, you can design and configure your processes and forms. ISR scenarios control the user interface in interactive forms in a form-based process. There is a 1:1 ISR Scenario–to–Form scenario relationship. Using ISR scenarios, you can define a set of form fields and properties (see Figure 2). For example, for a salary change the form scenario is defined with the Annual Salary field, which has a change property, and is a required field.

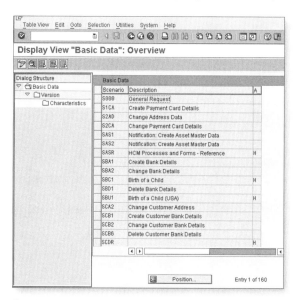

▲ *Figure 2* Change View Basic Data — Details

223

The Adobe Interactive Form connects the graphical user interface with the form scenario and provides for low complexity on form maintenance.

In the process, you can define the following elements: ISR scenario, Form scenario, workflow template, and initiator role (Manager Self-Service (MSS), HR Administrator). A process can include one or more Form scenarios. For example, in the Manager Change Requisition Required process, the initiating manager gets one form, the receiving manager gets a second form, and the finance manager receives a third form. All of these are different Form scenarios used in the same overall process (see Figure 3).

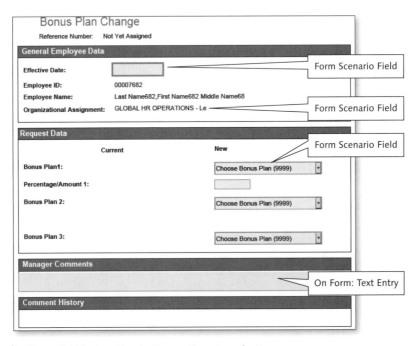

▲ **Figure 3** *Voluntary Termination — Overview of a Form*

In the workflow template, you can define the process flow, tasks, and agents to control the Form application in a process. You can define the steps in the process and who is involved in each step. Workflow is developed through the use of specific HCM P&F delivered workflow tasks in Transaction SWDD.

The process and forms for personnel actions such as transfer, promotions, demotions, lateral moves, return from leave, and termination can either be started by a manager or by an HR administrator using a start application. Basically, the start application consists of several views, including the Manager or HR Administrator view. You can initiate the start of a process, select the employee, and edit the form assigned to this process. You can then send the form for further processing. By sending this data, you end the start application and trigger the process that the system maps from this point in time using the form application. When the start application ends, you then trigger the selected process; this means that the system creates a workflow instance for the workflow template of the process. The execution of the start application is therefore the triggering event for the workflow of the process.

You can start the form and process by one of the following methods:

- Start application for HR Administrator
- Start application for Manager

These two applications differ only in terms of the Select Employee view: In the start application for the HR Administrator, this view includes a simple search and an enhanced search. The HR Administrator can select the employees to whom he is assigned. In the start application for managers, the manager can select the employees for whom he is responsible through the organizational assignment.

The start application for the Employee role is also executable. However, employees cannot see the SELECT EMPLOYEE view or the SELECT PROCESS view. An employee can only trigger processes for himself. The processes that are available are entered in the EMPLOYEE PORTAL ROLE in the LIFE AND WORK EVENTS area. Once a process has been selected, the employee is brought directly to the Edit view.

For more information about setting up the start application for employees, see the IMG for HR Administrative Services under RELATIONSHIPS TO OTHER ROLES • EMPLOYEE SELF-SERVICE.

Tip 78 Processing Multiple Employee's Records in Processes and Forms

You can use processes and forms to execute HR processes that require HR managers or administrators to make changes to multiple employees' HR Master Data using the Portal.

When your organization undergoes a major organizational restructuring or reduction in work force, mass transfers of employee data occurs. Managers often cannot make mass changes to their direct reports in MSS and have to either process one employee at a time, or depend on HR to complete the required processing. Using this tip, you can start a process for multiple employees at the same time in SAP Enterprise Resource Planning (ERP) HCM forms. The processes for multiple employees are divided into two categories: fast data entry and mass processes. Fast data entry is a one-step process with no work flow. A manager/HR administrator updates the data, and it's automatically saved in the backend. The mass update is a multistep process based on standard workflow-driven approval.

Solution

Managers can start the process for multiple employees in MSS by selecting the process and editing data in a table format. Data only appears in Form format in mass processes (when the next agent in the workflow opens the worklist item for one of the employees involved in the process).

To use this process, you need to have the customization set up in your system. To configure your process as a mass update process, follow these steps:

1. In Design Time for Processes and Forms, choose the process you want to configure.
2. Configure your process. For example, for a termination, do the required configuration for the termination process.
3. Assign the relevant roles by going to VALIDITY PERIOD • PROCESS START • ROLE ASSIGNMENT.

4. Add the relevant roles (e.g., HR Administrator), who can execute this process.

5. Design and configure the Form scenario. For example, in the termination process, you'll have a form that needs to be filled out by the manager, so this is where you configure the form tied to the termination process.

6. Design the workflow by selecting the workflow template.

Once configured as a mass process, you can then start this process in the Portal using START PROCESS FOR MULTIPLE EMPLOYEES, as shown in Figure 1.

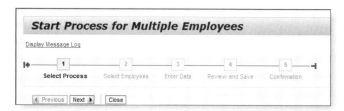

« Figure 1
Start Process for Multiple Employees

Here, you just have to select the process, and then select the employees for which you want to create mass processing. Then, just enter the data in the form, review, and save.

You'll receive a confirmation that the process is completed, as you can see in Figure 2, the IMG steps for forms and process configuration and DESIGN TIME FOR FORMS AND PROCESS design.

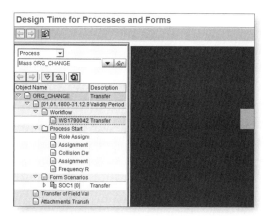

« Figure 2
Design Time for Processes and Forms

Simply complete the design and configuration of forms and process. To get to the Start Process for Multiple Employees, use the following menu path:

> PERSONNEL MANAGEMENT • HR ADMINISTRATIVE SERVICES • CONFIGURATION OF FORMS AND PROCESS • DESIGN TIME FOR FORMS AND PROCESS

Tip 79: Defining the Attachment Types Required for Your Form Scenario

You can define the attachments types for your forms and process scenarios. You can also make them optional or mandatory.

In your Adobe Forms and Process scenarios, attachments are used to provide additional information or supplement documents related to a particular process or form. Attachments are of greater importance based on the process' needs. You can differentiate between any information that a specifically classified process agent can add (in principle), and documents that are required for the business execution of a process. For example, the add a new born dependent process requires adding the birth certificate attribute and maternity leave requires adding the certificate of pregnancy attribute.

 Solution

The attachment type delivered in the standard system, general attachments (SFREE-ATTM), lets you add attachments that cannot be classified more precisely.

To start, use the following menu path:

> PERSONNEL MANAGEMENT • HR ADMINISTRATIVE SERVICES • CONFIGURATION OF FORMS AND PROCESSES • CONFIGURATION OF FORMS • CROSS FORMS SETTINGS • DEFINE ATTACHMENT TYPES

All other attachment types (delivered in the standard system or created by you) uniquely classify the attachment. They provide information about which document is to be provided when a process is executed. The system cannot check to see if the object provided is actually the required document. The standard system contains the following examples of attachment types:

- S7WEEKCRTF: 7 Weeks Certificate
- SBIRTHCRTF: Birth Certificate
- SHI1_WORK: Work Contract
- SPRGNYCRTF: Certificate of Pregnancy
- STN_RL: Reference
- STN_TL: Notice Letter of Employee
- SHIRE_FREE: Other Attachments for 'Hiring' Process
- SFREEATTM: General Attachments

You can use the ATTACHMENT TYPE if you want to offer the user the option of adding a (nonclassified) attachment of any kind to a process.

All attachment types are potentially available for all form scenarios/processes. You can create attachments in the IMG activity CREATE FORM SCENARIO under the ATTRIBUTES OF ATTACHMENT TYPES node (in the dialog structure under VERSIONS • SCENARIO STEPS), where you define which attachment type is actually used. You can also classify the attachment as optional or mandatory for relevant processing. You can now define the attachment types you need for your FORM SCENARIO, as shown in Figure 1.

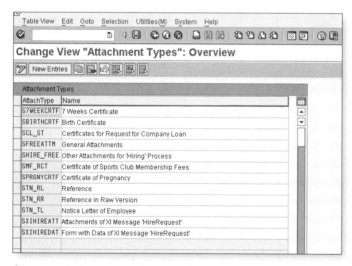

↥ *Figure 1* Change View Attachment Types — Overview

Part 12
HR Administrator Role

Things You'll Learn in this Section

80	Running a Free Text Search	232
81	Editing Employee Data in MSS from the Work Center	234
82	Using the Digital Personnel File to Simplify and Optimize HR Administrator	236
83	Using the HR Administrator Role for All Administrative HR Tasks	238

The HR Administrator Portal role provides all tasks and functions for the HR department in the Portal. It is integrated with the Processes and Forms framework. It supports the central processing of personnel data. You can also edit employee data in this role. The HR administrator can call the master data maintenance directly using employee data maintenance in the Portal or through the backend system. The HR administrator can change master data without using the HCM Processes and Forms framework. A benefit of the role is it also encourages decentralized execution of HR activities by including managers and employees (where necessary) directly in the process flow and thus reducing the workload for the HR department. This section of tips will help developers, business analysts, system administrators, and functional power-users in HR and IT to use the HR Administrator role in SAP ERP HCM in a more effective manner.

Tip 80: Running a Free Text Search

HR administrators can carry out their operations more efficiently using the HR Admin role in MSS. They can easily use free text search to find employee records.

HR administrators can run a free text search on an employee's forms, attachments, and infotype records. In infotypes, the system only searches the field labels and not the contents of the infotype fields. For example, Infotype 0002 — Personal Data — includes the Last Name field. Lopez is entered for an employee in this field. In this case, the system only displays a search result if the HR administrator enters Last Name as a search term. If the administrator uses Lopez as the search term, the system will not find anything.

For forms and attachments, however, the system searches both field labels and field contents. For example, a form includes the Last Name field. Lopez is entered for an employee in this field. In this case, the system searches both the field label Last Name and the field content Lopez for the search term.

The following reports need to be scheduled to run daily:

- Document class: DOCP03
- Document area: SRM
- Indicator: Index document area

Solution

The search is based on an iView that uses the Object and Data Provider (OADP) for employee searches and for displaying search results. To use this functionality, you must make the settings for the business package in HR Administrative Services by choosing IMG • HR ADMINISTRATOR • EMPLOYEE SEARCH.

To search using free text for employee records you need to log in to the Portal MSS and use the following the menu path:

> Portal • Manager Self Service • HR Administrator Role

As you can see in Figure 1, you can search any employees' record using the employees' last name, his personnel number, or his employee group, employee subgroup, or personnel area. You can search employee records in infotypes. If you check the infotype, the system will produce results that show all infotype records that have employees' data. You can also search employee records in Forms and in attachments by checking the FORMS and ATTACHMENTS checkboxes, as shown in Figure 2. This gives the HR administrator a quick way to search employee records using free text and review employee records.

⌃ *Figure 1* Find Processes

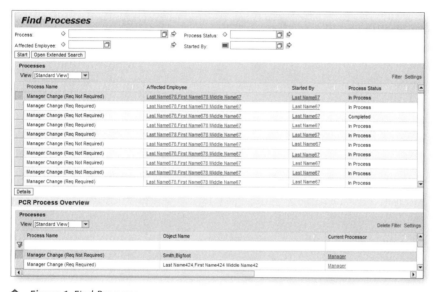

« *Figure 2*
Key Word Search

Tip 81: Editing Employee Data in MSS from the Work Center

You can use this function to access employee data directly in the Portal to create, edit, and display data using infotypes.

You can call the Edit Employee Data function directly from the work center for HR administrators. The user interface for editing employee data comprises the following areas:

- **Data selection:** Select an employee by entering the personnel number or the name of the employee. The name of the employee and the employee's data are displayed in the data maintenance area. The infotype browser is opened, and you can use Advanced Search to access other search functions.
- **Infotype browser:** This uses a tree structure that contains several nodes from which you can select an infotype or an action for processing. If no personnel number is selected in the data selection area, the infotype browser is empty. Once a personnel number is selected, the tree structure is displayed.
- **Data maintenance (and Infotype text):** In this area, you can display, create, or edit employee data. The system uses this data to create a history of all of the changes and developments pertaining to an employee during the period that the employee works at the company. You can also use this browser to navigate within the data maintenance area.

✓ Solution

Using the HR Administrator role, an HR analyst/administrator could maintain employee master data directly through the work center for HR administrators in MSS.

You can use the infotype browser to navigate within the data maintenance area. The following operations on infotypes are supported:

- Display Data Records
- Change Data Records
- Create Data Records

HR Administrator Role **Part 12**

- Copy Data Records
- Delete Data Records
- Lock/Unlock Data Records

As shown in Figure 1, you can select employee data records and click on START. You can then maintain employee data directly from the HR Administrator role. As shown in Figure 2, you can select infotypes for an employee via the INFOTYPE BROWSER and maintain employee data in infotypes. You can also execute Personnel Actions for an employee via the screen in Figure 2.

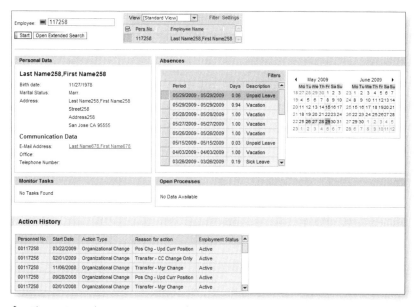

Figure 1 Employee Data — HR Administrator Role Work Center View

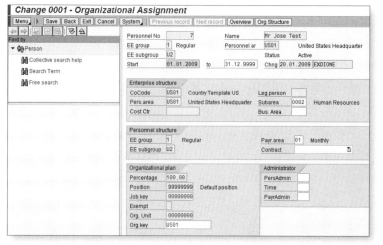

Figure 2
Employee Data —
Display Organizational Assignment

235

Tip 82 Using the Digital Personnel File to Simplify and Optimize HR Administrator

You can use the Digital Personnel File (DPF) to store central access to all employee documents for legal purposes.

The HR administrator can use the Digital Personnel Profile (DPP) iView to display an employee's DPF and make changes to it. The DPF can be used as a central repository for all the documents that affect your employees, such as documents relating to employment, remuneration, life events, or certificates and other legal documents. You can customize the structure of the DPF to meet your company's specific requirements.

There are two basic types of documents contained in the DPF:

- Process documents such as forms or attachments that result from an HCM Processes and Forms component process that has been executed for an employee.
- Archived documents that have already been stored manually by an HR administrator. The system will replace these documents using the personnel file instead of storing it in the DPF.

 Solution

The DPF can be populated with documents manually or by the system itself using processes within the framework of the HCM processes and forms component. If done by the system, it will automatically create the DPF for an employee at the completion of a process given appropriate authorization, an HR administrator can search, display, add, or delete documents, as well as display process forms and steps, as shown in Figure 1.

HR Administrator Role **Part 12**

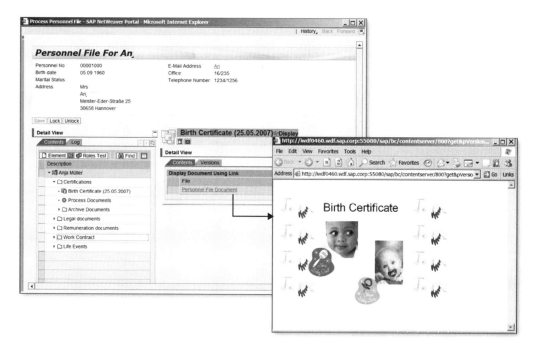

⌃ *Figure 1* Digital Personnel File

The DPF is an optimized HR Administrative Services (PA-AS) component. To use all the functions available through the DPF, you should also use the HCM Processes and Forms subcomponent from HR PA-AS. It is possible, however, to use the DPF by itself.

The DPF is based on SAP Records Management uses on the record model that structures the various folders of the DPF and decides which documents are stored in which folders. The DPF is also based on the one single record model that is required for all employees. Different record models cannot be used for different employee groups. To reach the Forms and Processes component, use the following menu path:

PORTAL • MANAGER SELF SERVICE • FORMS AND PROCESSES

Tip 83: Using the HR Administrator Role for All Administrative HR Tasks

You can use the HR Administrator role to perform all administrative tasks that relate to your employees' HR data that you normally perform through the SAP GUI.

Often, HR administrators had to work between the Portal and SAP GUI to perform their day-to-day SAP HR system-related tasks in older versions of SAP. This was very time-consuming and a difficult process. With the new HR Administrator role in ERP Central Component (ECC) 6.0 you can now have the HR administrator do all activities via the Portal easily and efficiently. All activities can be completed via one portal. Using the HR Administrator role in Manager Self-Service (MSS), you can perform all tasks that relate to the administration of SAP HR activities. You can carry out activities such as supporting, administering, and advising all employees in the relevant departments.

 Solution

The key areas covered under the HR Administrator role include:

Administering/editing personnel master data (i.e., new employees, hiring, termination, salary changes, organizational reassignments, administering leave of absences).

- Administering personnel appraisals
- Editing organizational data
- Performing year-end activities
- Providing statements and information
- Creating various reports required at different times
- Advising all employees, pensioners, and management

- Executing reports related to personnel administration activities (including anniversaries and birthdays) and assisting in the mass creation of benefit or compensation statements

The overview page for the HR administrator provides information about, and access to, the processes that he will be actively involved in supporting. First, use the following menu path:

> LOGIN IN TO ESS/MSS PORTAL • HR ADMINISTRATOR ROLE.

Once you log in, you will see the screen shown in Figure 1.

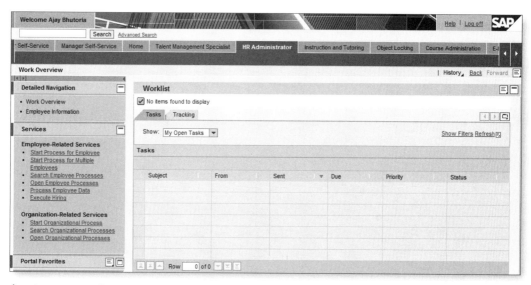

↑ **Figure 1** HR Administrator Work Overview

The HR administrator can also start and complete in-progress processes for a manager. The HR administrator also has more specific search capabilities to locate an employee than the manager. ■

Part 13
HR Security Authorization Management

Things You'll Learn in this Section

84	Controlling Employee Access to Self-Service Capabilities	242
85	Restricting Users from Viewing or Maintaining Their Own SAP ERP HCM Master Data	244
86	Accessing Users' SU53 Transaction from Your Own Desktop	246
87	Checking the Integrity of Data Entered in SAP ERP HCM	248

In HR, authorizations are critical because access to HR data must be strictly controlled. There are two primary ways to set up authorizations for SAP ERP HCM. First, you can set up general authorizations that are based on the general SAP authorization concept, or you can set up HR-specific structural authorizations that check by organizational assignment to see if a user is authorized to perform an activity. This section of tips will help developers, business analysts, system administrators, and functional power-users in HR and IT use security authorization management in SAP ERP HCM in a more effective manner.

Tip 84 — Controlling Employee Access to Self-Service Capabilities

You can use Employee Self-Services to control access and let your employees update their own master data.

All employees should be able to change their own address (Infotype 0006) and personnel data (Infotype 0002) using ESS in SAP ERP HCM. To do this, each employee should be authorized to access all master data stored under their personnel number. At the same time, the employees who don't have a HR Administrator role should not be able to access other employees' data. ESS gives you the ability to control employee access, where you can specify which infotypes employees should see.

✓ Solution

To enable employees to change their own master data, you can use Transaction PFCG or the following menu path. You will see the screens as shown in Figures 1 and 2.

> TOOLS • ADMINISTRATION USER MAINTENANCE • ROLE ADMINISTRATION ROLES

Next, you can take the following steps to allow users to change their own master data:

- Activate at least one of the authorization main switches (except for P_PERNR) to prevent users from accessing other personnel numbers. In this example, the AUTSW ORGIN main switch is the only active main switch. Also, the AUTSW PERNR main switch must be activated for the authorization check by personnel number to take place.
- Next, maintain the user assignment for all employees who use ESS in Infotype 0105. Every employee who uses ESS is granted the following two authorizations for the P_PERNR authorization object:

- AUTHC = R, M; PSIGN = I; INFTY = *; SUBTY = *
- AUTHC = *; PSIGN = I; INFTY = 0006,0002; SUBTY = *

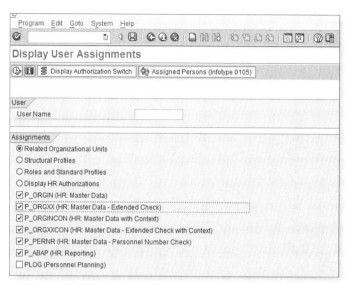

☆ *Figure 1* Role Maintenance

Select the ESS role that you want to maintain.

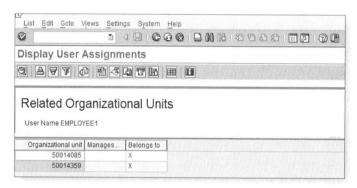

☆ *Figure 2* Display Role — Authorization

Figure 2 displays an ESS role giving authorization to Infotypes 0006 and 0021 on the Portal for an employee.

Tip 85: Restricting Users from Viewing or Maintaining Their Own SAP ERP HCM Master Data

Maintain data security and internal control by preventing administrators from maintaining their own data.

You can restrict HR administrators from maintaining their own data. For example, administrators responsible for the basic pay (Infotype 0008) of a personnel area (based on HR master data authorization) should be able to display their own data at all times, but not change their basic pay, regardless of the personnel area that they're responsible for. You'll need to set up the appropriate authorizations for the HR: Personnel Number Check object using Infotype 0008 — Basic Pay — records of all employees for a personnel area via P_ORGIN authorization. This is important because the Sarbanes-Oxley act (SOX) restricts users from maintaining their own data in systems related to basic pay, bonuses, salary increases, etc.

Solution

Authorizations for the authorization object P_PERNR must be set up as follows:

```
AUTHC(Authorization Level) = R, M
PSIGN = I
INFTY(Infotype) = *
SUBTY(Subtype) = *
AUTHC = W, S, D, E
PSIGN = E
INFTY = 0008
SUBTY = *
```

The first authorization grants the employee read authorization for all infotypes that are stored under the employee's personnel number. The second authorization denies write authorization for all data records of Infotype 0008 stored under the employee's personnel number. The authorization checks for all other personnel numbers and for write authorizations for all infotypes (except Infotype 0008) run according to P_ORGIN.

To restrict your users from maintaining their own data, you need to set up appropriate authorizations for the authorization object P_PERNR. Table 1 contains a description of authorization fields and values.

Authorization Field	Long Text
INFTY	Infotype
SUBTY	Subtype
AUTHC	Authorization Level
PERSA	Personnel Area
PERSG	Employee Group
PERSK	Employee Subgroup
VDSK1	Organizational Key

⌃ Table 1 Authorization Fields and Values

In addition, you can use the following:

- R (Read) for read access
- M (Matchcode) for read access to input helps [F4]
- W (Write) for write access
- E and D (Enqueue and Dequeue) for write access using the Asymmetrical Double Verification Principle. E allows the user to create and change locked data records and D allows the user to change lock indicators.
- S (Symmetric) for write access using the Symmetric Double Verification Principle

Select the ROLE for which you wish to restrict users from maintaining access or create a new role using the Create icon, as shown in Figure 1.

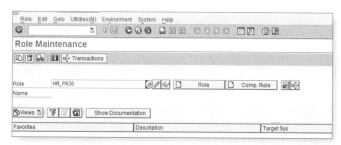

⌃ Figure 1 Role Maintenance

Tip 86: Accessing Users' SU53 Transaction from Your Own Desktop

You can access the screen display of your users' SU53 directly from your own desktop. This allows you to research or analyze authorization issues and guide the user accordingly.

Trying to access a transaction code and receiving an error message such as "You do not have authorization for Transaction X" is not an uncommon experience. It's easy for you to analyze the error in your own system by checking Transaction SU53. Authorization errors in other user's sessions, however, can't be analyzed as easily. Relying on your users to send screenshots of their Transaction SU53 results for troubleshooting is cumbersome and time-consuming. There is an alternative.

 Solution

You can ask the user to execute Transaction SU53 and then access the screen shot yourself using the Transaction SU53 on your own system. After the user executes Transaction SU53, you need to do the same and press F5 or click the CHOOSE USER icon at the top left of the screen. Type your user's ID to see their SU53 results screen. You will be able to see the user's details for SU53 so the user doesn't have to email you their screenshots. You can see it directly on your own screen and proceed to troubleshoot the problem. To do this, use the following menu path:

SYSTEM • UTILITIES • DISPLAY AUTHORIZATION

Use Transaction SU53. Click on the CHOOSE USER button at the top-left corner and enter the user ID of the person you want to get the screenshot from.

Click on DISPLAY AUTHORIZATION CHECK. It will bring you to the screen in Figure 1.

HR Security Authorization Management   Part 13

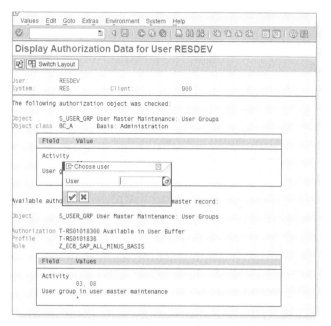

▲ Figure 1 Display Authorization Data for User RESDEV

Here, you can enter the user ID for whom you want to analyze the error. Once you enter the user ID and click Enter, you will see the SU53 screen of the other user. You can now review and analyze the error to resolve the user's access issue. Keep in mind, it's important that the user execute SU53 immediately after they receive the error, so it will relate to the error in question (see Figure 2).

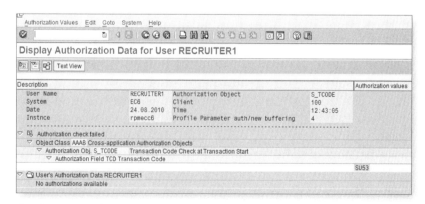

▲ Figure 2 Display Authorization Data for User ARM

247

Tip 87 Checking the Integrity of Data Entered in SAP ERP HCM

You can control and check the integrity of data entered in SAP ERP HCM by using test procedures.

You can define whether the system should execute control checks for infotypes using a test procedure. You can also define those infotypes (and their subtypes) for which control checks should be carried using a test procedure. This test procedure function for infotypes is particularly useful when the system needs to check the integrity of data entered by employees. For example, Employee X enters his own time data in the system. The absence and attendance data should go through a control test procedure. Employee X must have the authority to write to infotypes that are relevant to time recording and must also have the authority to read the test procedures (Infotype 0130). He can only enter time data for the period after it has been released following a test procedure.

Manager Y, who is Employee X's superior, has the authority to write to the infotypes that are relevant to time recording and the infotypes that are relevant to the test procedures (Infotype 0130). At the end of a time evaluation period, she checks the data using a time evaluation report and releases it. The release date is automatically set to the date at the end of the period checked. Employee X cannot change any data for the previous period. Manager Y, however, can still change data records that have been released.

 Solution

Normally, you process the test procedures (Infotype 0130) using a program. You can also process it manually using Transaction PA30. For the customizing steps, use the menu path, as shown in Figure 1.

> PERSONNEL ADMINISTRATION • CUSTOMIZING: TOOLS • AUTHORIZATION ADMINISTRATION • SPECIAL AUTHORIZATIONS IN PERSONNEL ADMINISTRATION • TEST PROCEDURES • CREATE TEST PROCEDURES OR ASSIGN INFOTYPES TO TEST PROCEDURES

You can process test procedures as shown in Figure 2 using report RPTAPPU0. This is a master report that implements a control for a test procedure for time infotype records that have already been entered.

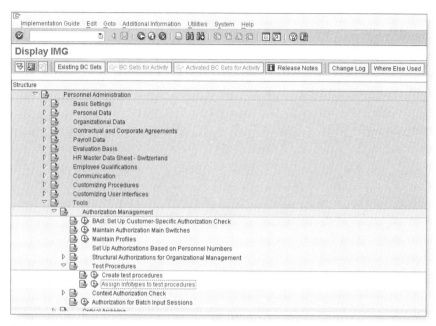

⌃ *Figure 1* Display IMG

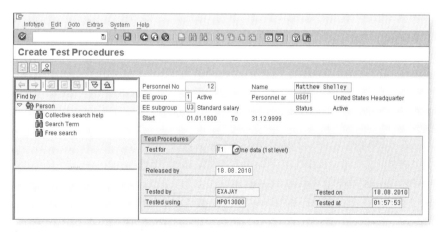

⌃ *Figure 2* Create Test Procedures (Infotype 0130)

Part 14

Reporting

Things You'll Learn in this Section

88	Comparing Two Security Roles to Maintain Your Authorizations and SOX Compliance	252
89	Improving the Performance of Your Reports and Queries Using Dynamic Selections	254
90	Executing Reports from the MSS Launch Pad	258
91	Executing HR Reports Using Structural Display	260
92	Using QuickViewer to Create Basic List Reports for Occasional HR and Payroll Users	262
93	Transporting Reports Developed in the SAP Query Standard Area from One System to Another	266

Human Resources (HR) management requires complete and current information on employees in the company. SAP ERP HCM contains all relevant employee data for analysis and decision-making processes. To enable you to report on HR data, the SAP system provides you with numerous standard reports and, in addition, reporting tools that give you easy access to existing reports (HIS) or enable you to create your own reports, even if you have no programming skills (InfoSet Query, SAP Query). This section of tips will help developers, business analysts, system administrators, and functional power-users focused on SAP ERP HCM how to use the reporting tools and capabilities in a more efficient and effective manner.

Tip 88: Comparing Two Security Roles to Maintain Your Authorizations and SOX Compliance

You can compare security roles to identify differences and maintain your SOX compliance.

When you are working with multiple security roles you may not always know the differences between the roles. Now you can easily compare two roles and identify those differences for a better understanding. This can be especially useful, for example, if you are creating Parent and Child roles. You can compare the differences between the roles and adjust them accordingly.

You can also compare the same role across environments — Development, Quality, and Production — in your system landscape. This is really helpful when your systems are out of sync during upgrades, or if ongoing role maintenance has been done in Production or Quality without updating Development. It's important to note, though, that you must maintain Remote Function Call (RFC) destinations between two systems to compare two role menus from those systems.

You can easily use this process to compare role menus that belong to:

- Two roles in an SAP system
- Two roles in different SAP systems
- A role and its template
- A newly delivered role and its previous customer version

✓ Solution

To compare the role menus, use the display mode by clicking the Compare button. To adjust the menu of the first role, that is, to copy parts of the comparison role menu, you can change the mode by clicking Adjust. The procedure describes the change mode.

In the role maintenance (Transaction PFCG), choose UTILITIES then the ROLE COMPARISON tool or call Transaction ROLE_CMP. Enter the name of the role to be adjusted in the ROLE INPUT field. Then enter the comparison role in the COMPARISON ROLE field. First, use the following menu path:

> ENVIRONMENT • ROLE COMPARISON TOOL IN ROLE MAINTENANCE

As shown in Figure 1, you can enter the name of the role to be compared in the ROLE input field. From here, enter the COMPARISON ROLE, and press Enter, which will bring you to Figure 2.

« *Figure 1*
Compare and Adjust Roles

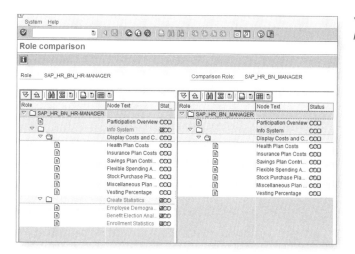

« *Figure 2*
Role Comparison

Some of the entries in the menu of the roles to be compared are output in red. This means that the entries in red have been added in comparison with the role Role_Compare_2. You can select and delete these entries if you want to keep these roles in sync. You can also drag and drop and copy these missing entries into role 2. ■

Tip 89: Improving the Performance of Your Reports and Queries Using Dynamic Selections

Dynamic selections enhance the usefulness of your reports and improve the efficiency of reports and queries.

The Dynamic Selection functionality is used to limit the selection of data by a query or report. Dynamic selections enhance the usefulness of a report because you can add fields (data) to the report results using selection criteria that are not included in the standard selection screen of the logical database. You can do this without having to make changes to the report program. This is done via assigning the report to a report category.

Dynamic selections improve the performance of your reports and queries by adding conditions that return smaller, more specific data sets more quickly. Dynamic selections are more effective than when selection fields are added during query definition. For example, if you are using your SAP ERP HCM system to create reports for a fictitious company of 12,000 employees, you're most likely using queries to create reports on different subsets of employees. In our example, you might want to report on Latin America and only 300 of your employees satisfy this condition. Assuming you use this condition as your only selection criterion, you can see the difference in performance with and without dynamic selections. Without dynamic selections, data (persons) is retrieved in two steps. First, all 12,000 employees are read from the database and transferred to your program. Second, the 300 employees in question are selected from these 12,000 employees. With dynamic selections, your condition is transferred straight to the database. Just 300 employees are read from the database, and transferred to your program. This more effective method of accessing data improves performance considerably. It often enables you to execute reports and queries directly which, without dynamic selections, could only be executed in batch operations.

Solution

To include dynamic selections in your reports and queries, use the steps outlined in the following, starting with this menu path (also see Figure 1):

TOOLS • ABAP WORKBENCH • OVERVIEW • OBJECT NAVIGATOR

1. You need to enter the development class in the Development class field, to which the selection view must be assigned (in this example, we use the customer development class).
2. Next, choose EDIT OBJECT and select the SELECTION view.
3. Choose the Create icon and select FOR ANY TABLES, and enter a name that starts with PNP in the NAME OF VIEW field and press Enter.
4. In the Tables dialog box, enter the database tables of the infotypes from which the fields for your dynamic selections are taken (for example, PA0006 for infotype 2) and press Enter.
5. In the Functional group box, enter a number and name for the functional group (for example, 01 and Dynamic Selections). You can group your dynamic selections together in a functional group, or you can group them together by infotype. If you choose the latter option, dynamic selections are sorted by infotype when queries are executed.
6. In the TABLES/NODES GROUP box, select an infotype for processing by double-clicking on it.
7. If you want a field to be available immediately as a dynamic selection when a query is executed, select its PRESELECTION checkbox.
8. If fields are not included in the preselection, you can use them as dynamic selections as required, and click Save.
9. Access Customizing for the Human Resources Information System by using the following menu path:

TOOLS • ACCELERATEDSAP • CUSTOMIZING • EDIT PROJECT • SAP REFERENCE IMG: PERSONNEL MANAGEMENT • HUMAN RESOURCES INFORMATION SYSTEM

Tip 89   *Improving the Performance of Your Reports and Queries Using Dynamic Selections*

10. Choose REPORTING • ADJUSTING THE STANDARD SELECTION SCREEN • CREATE REPORT CATEGORIES.

11. Create a report category. When you do so, enter the name of the selection view that you created in the Name of selection view field.

12. Save your report category. You can now use your selection view in the new report category.

↟ *Figure 1 ABAP Development Workbench*

You can create your report categories and assign report-to-report categories, as shown in Figures 2 and 3.

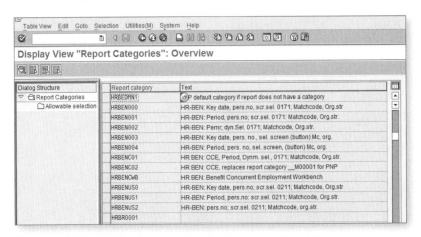

↟ *Figure 2 Display View Report Categories: Overview – Report Category*

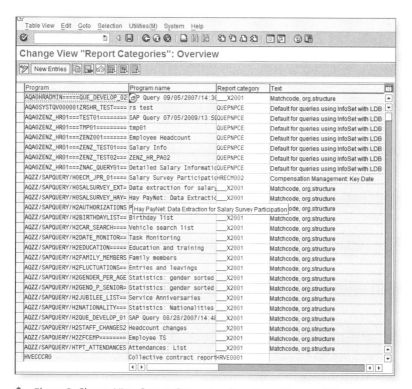

▲ *Figure 3 Change View Report Categories: Overview – Program Lists*

Tip 90: Executing Reports from the MSS Launch Pad

Managers can use the Reporting Launch pad to easily select and execute HR or cross-functional reports from MSS.

Often, managers get confused or spend too much time trying to find reports in MSS. The experience can be frustrating and managers often resort to calling HR to execute the report. This is inefficient for everyone involved. You can avoid this problem and organize your reporting in MSS using the Reporting Launch pad iView. The launch pad can serve as a single point of access to all. The reports are organized by categories (that can be tailored to meet specific needs) during customization. This will make it easier for managers to find and launch the desired report. You can allow a list of suitable reports to users in the role "manager" to be used by the manager. Your managers can rearrange this list to meet their own requirements, adding their own folders and changing the order of the reports as they see fit.

 Solution

You can configure the HCM reports based on entries in the Manager's Desktop (MDT) tables. Entries from MDT tables can be transferred to the launch pad tables to let managers execute the reports via Launch pad. You need to complete the Implementation Guide (IMG) activity Convert MDT Data to MSS Reporting launch pad using the scenario RPT0.

As shown in Figure 1, you can organize reports using a number of cross-functional areas such as TEAMS, BUDGET, PROJECTS, EMPLOYEE DATA, and so on. You can include a link to the report and provide explanatory text to assist managers with finding the right report. Once a report is opened, a selection screen will appear for the user to specify conditions or filters on results. Once executed, the report output is displayed in the next window as a Web GUI result list.

Reporting   Part 14

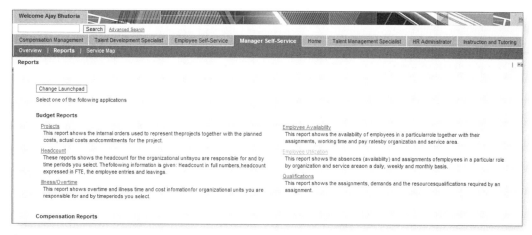

⇗ Figure 1 Launch Pad Reports

In the standard delivery, a manager can access the Launch pad iView by choosing the following path in the Top Level Navigation (TLN) part of the SAP Enterprise Portal:

(MANAGER SELF SERVICE • REPORTS)

In the Reporting Launch pad, you can display a scorecard element from SEM–CPM. You can also display myStaff reports and myBudgets reports in one page in Launch pad reports. You can also change the MDT reports to Launch pad reports. All other management reports can be added to Report Launch pad via customization. You can organize your reports by folders in Launch pad and you can also personalize reports in Launch pad.

To start a report from the Launch pad example, start the Birthday report using the Lauch pad iView. Under the EMPLOYEE DATA category, you can find A BIRTHDAY link. Click on it and launch it. You can then select the employees you want to execute this report for.

A new window opens and shows the result list. The result list shows reports as a Web GUI result list.

259

Tip 91: Executing HR Reports Using Structural Display

You can use the SAP ERP HCM reporting tool Human Information Systems (HIS) to perform reporting in a more visual, simplified, and efficient manner.

You can execute HR reports by using a very simple standard reporting tool — HIS. This tool allows you to start reports directly from structural graphics without having to enter data in a selection screen. In HIS, however, the system sets the required selection parameter based on those most commonly used. This is a very efficient method of setting selection parameters and can always be changed to meet your current needs.

The best part of using HIS is that it enables you to start a report from the selection screen. The reports in HIS are displayed in different categories, such as Benefits, Payroll, and Personnel Administration. You don't have to switch applications or follow any confusing menu paths or remember transaction codes.

 Solution

You can execute a report in HIS using two windows select an object using structural graphics in the first, and you'll see a list of available reports in the second.

To execute a report in HIS, use the following menu path:

> HUMAN RESOURCES • INFORMATION SYSTEM • REPORTING TOOLS • HIS

In the initial screen of HIS, shown in Figure 1, you can select the standard entry in the view fields of the module that you want to execute reports for.

You can select the required display option for structural graphics in the GRAPHICS DISPLAY GROUP box. The object or the organizational unit you select here will be the root object for the report. In the ORGANIZATIONAL UNIT field, enter the organizational structure that must be displayed, and click Execute. You will see that the structural graphics and reporting screen is displayed. The upper section of this screen lets you determine the areas within HR from which reports are offered. The list of available reports is displayed in the lower task function section.

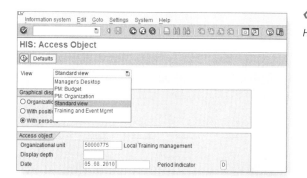

« Figure 1

HIS — Access Object

You can select an ORGANIZATIONAL UNIT, POSITION, or a PERSON in structural graphics and double-click on the TASK FUNCTIONS section. You'll see the output of the report displayed, as shown in Figure 2. You can download the report to Excel as well.

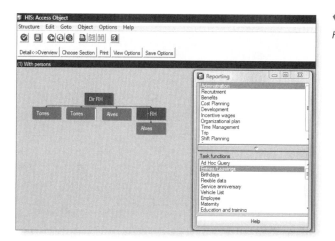

« Figure 2

HIS — Access Object 0074

Figure 3 displays the output for the report showing the employees hired with their hiring date and employees leaving with their termination date.

« Figure 3

HIS — Entries and Leaving

Tip 92 Using QuickViewer to Create Basic List Reports for Occasional HR and Payroll Users

You can use QuickViewer to provide existing, infrequent, or even new users with self-serve access to predefined or simple user-defined HR and Payroll reports.

SAP Query is a reporting tool in SAP ERP HCM that offers the user a wide range of options for defining reports. SAP Query also supports different kinds of reports, such as basic lists, statistics, and ranked lists. QuickViewer is a tool for generating simple reports. It provides even inexperienced or new users a way to define and create basic lists. QuickViewer possess the same functional attributes as queries, however, you can only create basic lists. You can transfer a QuickView into SAP Query to make reports accessible to additional users, or to use the other functions available in SAP Query.

You don't need to make any user group assignments as is the case with Queries. Each user defines their own user-specific QuickViews that only they can display. This means that you cannot copy other users' QuickViews. You can, however, compile an SAP Query from a QuickView, if the QuickView uses a functional area from the standard system as a data source. The query is then visible to the user group.

You do not need Infosets to define a QuickView. When you define a QuickView, you need to specify its data source explicitly. Tables, database views, table joins, logical databases, and even InfoSets, can all serve as data sources for a QuickView. And, it's important to remember that you can only use additional tables and additional fields if you use an InfoSet as a data source. Certain hardware and software requirements must be fulfilled before you can use the QuickViewer.

Solution

To define a QuickView, you select specific fields according to your data source to determine the structure of your report. The report can be executed in basis mode with a standard layout.

To start, use the following menu path:

> SYSTEM • SERVICES • QUICKVIEWER

You can select QuickViewer from the table control on your initial screen or by entering its name in the appropriate input field (see Figure 1). You can now create your own basic list report (see Figure 2).

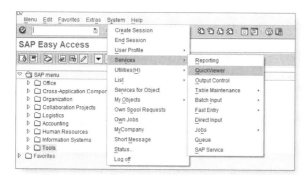

« *Figure 1*
SAP Easy Access

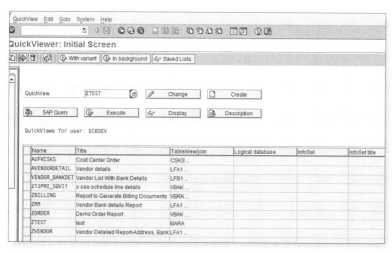

⌃ *Figure 2* Quick Viewer — Initial Screen

Click the Create icon to create your basic list report (see Figure 3).

Tip 92 Using QuickViewer to Create Basic List Reports for Occasional HR and Payroll Users

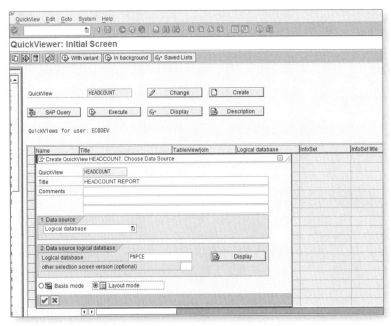

△ *Figure 3* *Quick Viewer — Initial Screen*

Enter the Logical database PNPCE (see Figure 4).

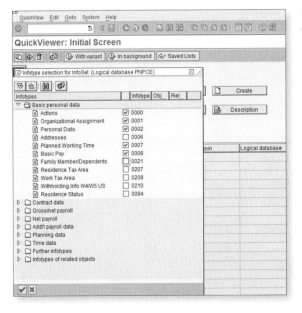

《 *Figure 4*
Quick Viewer — Initial Screen

You can select the infotypes. In the next step, you can select the fields from the infotype to be displayed in the output of your report (see Figure 5). You can then execute the report (see Figure 6). You will get the desired output. You can save your report as a variant for future use. This was a very simple and easy way to create your own basic lists.

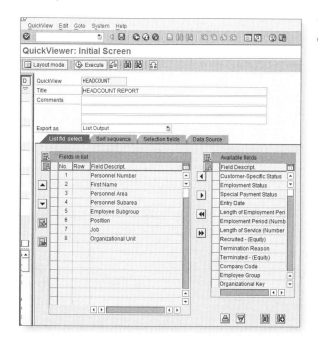

« *Figure 5*
Quick Viewer — Initial Screen

« *Figure 6*
Head Count Report

Enter the Selection details and click Execute to see the report output. ■

Tip 93: Transporting Reports Developed in the SAP Query Standard Area from One System to Another

You can transport queries and reports developed using SAP Query in the standard area from one system to another. This will keep all of the systems synchronized with each other and helps to meet Sarbanes-Oxley (SOX) compliance requirements.

Many users create SAP queries in a standard area in each environment of their system landscape (e.g., Development, Quality, and Production). Maintaining these queries consistently across systems requires time and effort and if not done methodically, may lead to synchronization issues. Using the SAP Query Transport Tool, you can transport the queries in a standard area from one source system to another target system and save considerable time and effort. You can also copy query objects from the standard area to the global area (or from the global area to the standard area).

When you create your query objects in the standard area, they are not automatically included in a transport package, so you'll need to transport them using the query transport tool. In the following Solution, you'll learn on how to transport query objects from a source system to a target system.

Solution

Transporting a query from a source (e.g., Development) to a target system (e.g., Quality) is a two-step process. First is creating the transport and second is importing the transport manually. This, of course, is assuming that you'll have the necessary authorizations to execute the following steps. To start, use Transaction SQ02, or use the following menu path:

> Tools • ABAP Workbench • Utilities • SAP Query • Infosets

To start, create a Data Set Request/Transport from the source system by taking the following steps:

1. Go to Environment and change the Query Area to Standard Area (client-specific)
2. Click on the Transport button
3. In the SAP Query Transport Tool, select the Transport radio button and check the following boxes:
    - Transport Query Variants (only with export/import/copy)
    - Transport of Query Layout Variants (only for export/import/copy)
    - Transport the report interface for queries (only with export/import)
4. Select the Transport Infosets and Queries radio button and include the names of the Infoset and Query to be transported
5. Click Execute

The next step in the process is to transport a query from one system to another and importing to your target system. Go to Environment and change the Query Area to Standard Area (client-specific):

1. Click on the Transport button
2. In SAP Query: Transport Tool, select the Import radio button, and check the following boxes:
    - Overwriting Allowed
    - Transport Query Variants (only with export/import/copy)
    - Transport of Query Layout Variants (only for export/import/copy)
    - Transport the report interface for queries (only with export/import)

Tip 93 Transporting Reports Developed in the SAP Query Standard Area from One System to Another

3. Select the TRANSPORT INFOSETS AND QUERIES radio button and include the name of the INFOSET and QUERY to be transported.
4. Include the DATA SET REQUEST NO. created in Step 1 in the DATA SET with the Imports option.
5. Click Execute (see Figure 1).

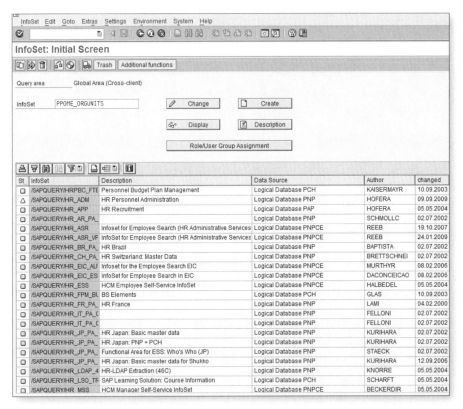

⚠ *Figure 1 Infoset — Initial Screen*

In Figure 1, you can select the QUERY you want to include in the transport. If you know the name of the QUERY, you can enter it or you can use the drop down menu to see the complete list.

Enter the QUERY NAME and click Execute. You will have your query included in the Transport. Now, as per the previous steps, you can go to the next client and import the transport to import your query to another client (see Figure 2).

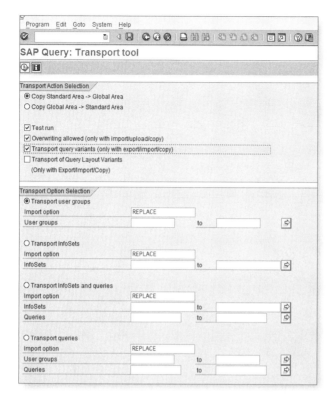

Figure 2
SAP Query — Transport Tool

You can execute test run to make sure your data entered is correct, and then you can execute by unchecking the TEST RUN and entering data as in Figure 2. You can then go to the next client and import your query. You can now execute the query in the next client and see the out put of query.

Part 15

Miscellaneous

Things You'll Learn in this Section

94	Translating Your Organizational Structure into Multiple Languages	272
95	Creating Standard and Structural Authorization Profiles and Roles	274
96	Displaying Long Text on Infotypes	276
97	Transporting Your Organizational Structure Manually	278
98	Using Transaction Codes to Access HR IMG Nodes	280
99	Creating Custom Transaction Codes for Your Day-to-Day HR Activities	282
100	Creating a Mini Information Board on the SAP GUI Log-On Screen	284

This section of tips will help the developer, business analyst, system administrator, and functional power-user in HR and IT use SAP ERP HCM more effectively. You'll gain insights across a number of areas, including:

- Translating multiple records on the same screen into multiple languages
- Using Long Text on your infotypes to help users understand the master data values better
- Transporting organizational structures, relationships, and objects through your system landscape to save time, money, and avoid complex conversions
- Saving the transaction codes as favorites in your SAP Favorites
- Using Transaction SE16 with organizational structure, relationships, and objects to create custom transaction codes and assign them to access the tables or reports directly
- Displaying customized information related to the system, log on clients, key dates, or help desk contact information on your SAP log-on screen
- Creating custom transaction codes and assigning them to access the tables or reports directly rather than using ad hoc queries via Transaction SE16

Tip 94: Translating Your Organizational Structure into Multiple Languages

You can translate multiple records on the same screen for Infotypes 1001 (Objects) and 1002 (Description) into multiple languages using the standard report RHTRANSO.

You can translate the organizational structure and objects in Infotype 1000 into multiple languages by maintaining one record at a time or via data upload using a custom program. This is a time-consuming and inefficient method. You can translate multiple records on the same screen for Infotype 1000 and Infotype 1002 into multiple languages on the same screen using the standard Translate Language Dependent Records report (RHTRANSO), which we'll discuss in the following Solution.

Solution

Report RHRTRANSO lets you translate language-dependent texts and all existing subtypes of Infotype 1000 and Infotype 1002. You can enter data in the selection screen and execute the report. On the output list screen, you can translate language-dependent texts into one or more languages and edit or delete the existing translations. Once you have translated the texts, you will see them displayed automatically in the appropriate language when you log on in the translated language.

To translate the text in Infotype 1000, you can use the following menu path:

> ORGANIZATIONAL MANAGEMENT • TOOLS • INFOTYPE • TRANSLATE

Enter data in the selection screen, as shown in Figure 1. Select the objects that you want to translate records for in Infotypes 1000 and 1002. You will also need to specify the language you want to translate the dependent texts into. In this example, the log-in language is English and the target language is Portuguese. Execute the report.

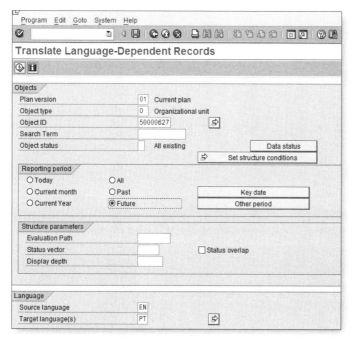

☆ *Figure 1* Translate Language — Dependent Records

You will see the results shown in Figure 2. For each language-dependent record of Infotype 1000, fields that are ready for input are displayed in the Abbreviation (ABBR) and OBJECT ID columns for each target language. In these fields, you can translate the source text or edit existing translations.

☆ *Figure 2* Translate Language — Dependent Records

Tip 95: Creating Standard and Structural Authorization Profiles and Roles

You can use report RHPROFL0 to create standard authorization profiles and role assignments for users in an organizational structure.

Report RHPROFL0 allows you to create authorization profile assignments for users based on organizational structure. Using this report, you make a distinction between standard authorization profiles and authorization profiles for structural Personnel Development (PD) authorizations. In addition, user roles and their profiles are assigned to the user.

 Solution

You can save all users in the structure using the start evaluation path PROFL0. Starting from these users on a key date, the system reads all valid related objects for which Infotypes 0106 (Standard Authorization Profile) or 1017 (Authorization Profile for Structural PD Authorizations) are maintained, up to the next highest organizational unit. This means that the superior organizational units are not taken into account.

The report includes all of the relevant object types such as job (C), position (S), organizational unit (O), task (T), task group (TG), workflow template (WS), workflow task (WF), standard task (TS), work center (A), and responsibilities (RY). This also includes all user roles (AG) and their standard authorizations. The system then checks to see if the users found are already created in the system. This is necessary because in Infotype 0105 (subtype 0001) of a person, users can be entered that are not created in the system. If a user is not yet in the system, it is automatically created. Then the system enters authorization profiles for all users found in the organizational plan.

You can validate the results for the standard authorization profiles and user roles using Transaction SU01, while you can display the structural PD authorizations using Transaction OOSB.

In the following steps, you'll learn how to enter the reporting parameters.

- Start the object. In this section, the Evaluation path searches the organizational plan for all assigned users. You can also specify a specific user in the start object so only a specific user is selected. In addition, you can specify a key date for the evaluation for the relationships to be done. Select the Test run parameter to have the system identify and evaluate the authorization profiles, without assigning them to the corresponding users.
- Generate authorization profiles. You can set Generate standard authorizations parameter to change the corresponding standard authorization profiles.

You can execute this report using Transaction SE38 and selecting report RHPROFL0.

Execute the report by entering the required data in the selection parameters, as shown in Figure 1.

« *Figure 1*
Generate User Authorizations

Enter the data in the selection screen and click Execute. ■

Tip 96 Displaying Long Text on Infotypes

The descriptions available for displaying long text in your infotypes will help your users understand the master data values better and perform your work more effectively.

If you don't have long text turned on, and you are using transactions such as PA30 to access master data, you will see HR infotype attributes displayed without Long Text. For example, you would see Personnel Area US01 with no description of what US01 means. You can easily display the long text associated with infotypes by customizing the IMG for infotypes that don't automatically default to long text. By displaying the long text, users can understand the details behind master data values better and do their work more efficiently without memorization.

 Solution

To maintain long text, you can execute an IMG customization or use table V T582A. You can select the infotype you want to maintain and select TEXT ALLOWED by using the following menu path (Figure 1):

> SPRO • PERSONNEL MANAGEMENT • PERSONNEL ADMINISTRATION–CUSTOMIZING PROCEDURE

By turning on this feature you have turned on long text. If you go back to Transaction PA30 and select this infotype, you will see long text being displayed, as shown in Figure 2.

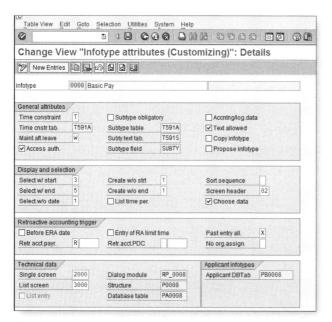

⌃ *Figure 1* Change View Infotype Attributes (Customizing)

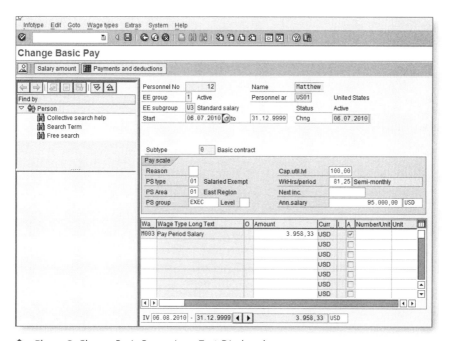

⌃ *Figure 2* Change Basic Pay — Long Text Displayed

Tip 97 Transporting Your Organizational Structure Manually

You can save time and money, and avoid complex conversions when creating your organizational structure, relationships, and objects. You can easily transport them from your development system to the rest of your system landscape using report RHMOVE30.

Many users re-create their organizational structures in each environment across their system landscape — Development, Quality, and Production. This practice requires a lot of time, resources, and effort in data load, conversions, and validation of data. In addition, it can also introduce inconsistencies across the different environments.

As an alternative, you can use the standard report RHMOVE30 to create manual transports for organizational structures or Personnel Development (PD)/Organizational Management (OM) objects. You can then release the transports for import and apply them to the other systems.

 Solution

To manually transport your PD/OM objects or organizational structure, you need to use report RHMOVE30. As shown in Figure 1, if you want to transport the entire organizational structure and all its relationships, including positions, chief position relationships, relationships to cost center, and so on, you can create one transport based on the selection screen by selecting the object O for all reporting periods, and apply the transport to the rest of your system landscape. To get to report RHMOVE30, you can use Transaction SE38 and select the report.

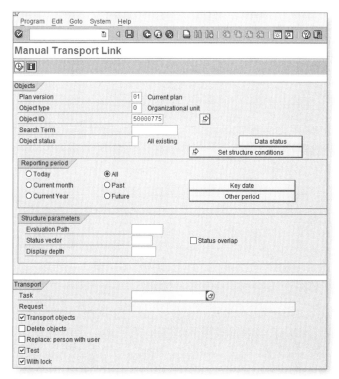

⌃ *Figure 1 Manual Transport Link*

As shown in Figure 2, you can save the entries in a transport. From here, you can release the transport for import and apply it to your Quality and/or Production systems.

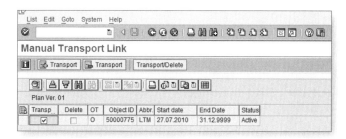

⌃ *Figure 2 Manual Transport Link*

Tip 98 Using Transaction Codes to Access HR IMG Nodes

You can save the transaction codes in your SAP Favorites, which will allow you to access your HR IMG nodes quickly.

The IMG menu path is often confusing and can be a significant a challenge to remember if you are not a frequent user. Drilling down the long IMG menu path to the specific step you need to update a configuration can be very time-consuming.

There is a simple process, however, to access the IMG steps using transaction codes in the same way that you maintain master data using Transaction code PA30. In the following Solution, you'll learn how.

You can create a setting in IMG that will display the transaction codes for each IMG step in the menu path. The next time you want to access a specific IMG step, just type the transaction code instead of going through transaction SPRO. Saving those frequently used transaction codes in your SAP "favorites" is a real time saver.

 Solution

To activate the setting, go to Transaction SPRO and display the IMG screen (as shown in Figure 1). On the top menu bar click ADDITIONAL INFORMATION and select the submenu ADDITIONAL INFORMATION. From the submenu, click on DISPLAY KEYS, and then IMG ACTIVITY. In Figure 2, you can see the ADDITIONAL INFORMATION (transaction codes for each step) displayed along with the IMG steps.

The IMG steps are displayed along with the transaction codes. For example, if you visit the IMG step CREATE Form of ADDRESS in Personnel Management very often, instead of having to remember the IMG path, you can use Transaction OHX0020. The transaction code is displayed next to the IMG, as shown in Figure 2, and is easier to use.

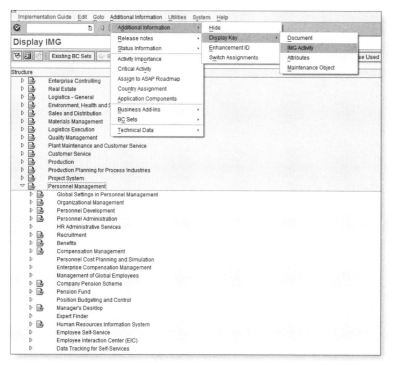

⌃ *Figure 1* Display IMG: IMG Activity

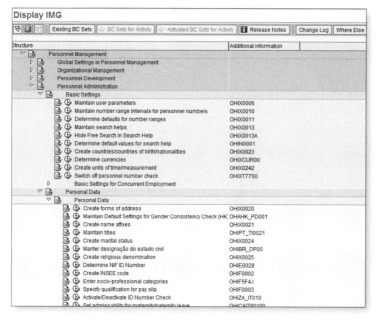

《 *Figure 2*
Display IMG:
Personal Data

Tip 99 Creating Custom Transaction Codes for Your Day-to-Day HR Activities

If you use an ad hoc query or access tables via Transaction SE16 frequently, you can create custom transaction codes and assign them to access the tables or reports directly.

The need to access various HR tables to download or review data frequently is common across most organizations. For example, you may need to look at table HRP1001 (Relationships). This table is usually accessed via Transaction SE16. There is an easier way, however, to access this table. You can now create and assign a transaction code to access this table directly. Similarly, if you are frequently accessing ad hoc query reports you can create a transaction code and assign it to the reports.

In addition to simplifying your access, these custom transaction codes can be built into your security roles to further control data access. You don't have to give your key HR users access to Transaction SE16 and table HRP1000, instead just provide access to the transaction codes. It's best, however, to keep the name of the transaction code simple and intuitive. To get started, follow the steps as in the following Solution.

✓ Solution

This solution shows you how to create a new transaction code and assign it to a table or report. In this example, you'll assign table HRP1001 to a new transaction code with same name as table HRP1001. Take the following steps:

1. Use Transaction SE93 to create a new transaction and define it as a parameter transaction, as you can see in Figure 1.
2. Enter SE16 into the Transaction field and select the Skip initial screen checkbox, as shown in Figure 2.

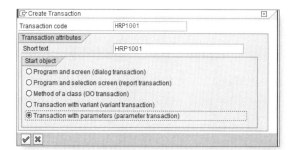

« *Figure 1*
Create Transaction

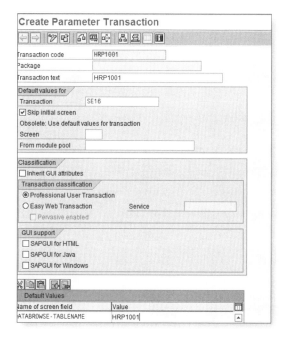

« *Figure 2*
Create Parameter Transaction

3. On the lower portion of the screen, enter the following information:
   ▸ NAME OF SCREEN FIELD: DATABROWSE-TABLENAME
   ▸ VALUE: Enter the name of the table you want to browse with SE16
4. When you save these entries, you will be prompted to add this change to a development class and transport. Use development class ZSEC for security or any other development class recommended by the development team.
5. Add the changes into a transport request and map the new transaction to an authorization object with Transaction SU24.
6. Find out with Transaction SE54 what authorization group the table(s) belongs to.

Execute Transaction HRP1001, and you will be able to access table HRP1001 directly via this transaction code. ■

Tip 100: Creating a Mini Information Board on the SAP GUI Log-On Screen

You can display customized information, such as details related to the system, log-on clients, key dates, or help desk contact information on your SAP log-on screen.

You can display specialized information on the SAP log-on screen for your users, including which clients (such as Development, QA, Production or Demo) are available, names of the clients, descriptions of clients, system outage messages and times, contact information for the help desk, and so on. When a user logs in to the SAP system, they can see the screen with all of the details on the mini bulletin board. You can easily update the text as frequently as needed via the following Solution.

 Solution

To display information on your bulletin board, you need to complete the following steps.

1. Access Transaction code SE61.
2. Select Document Class General Text, as shown in Figure 1.
3. Enter ZLOGIN_SCREEN_INFO, as shown in Figure 2.
4. Change the text as you want it to display on the SAP log-in screen, as shown in Figure 3.

For example, you can add the information about different systems available, such as development, quality, training, and demo clients. You can change the text as you want to display on the screen on a regular basis, to keep the system information up to date for users.

Miscellaneous **Part 15**

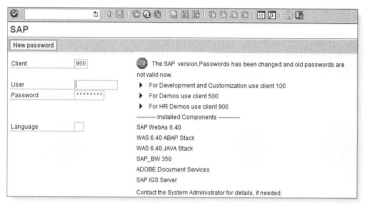

⭡ *Figure 1 SAP Log-on Screen*

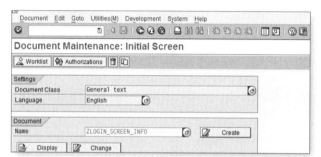

« *Figure 2*
Document Maintenance —
Initial Screen

« *Figure 3*
Change General
Text — ZLOGIN_SCREEN_INFO
Language EN

Additional Resources

SAP Service Marketplace

The SAP Service Marketplace is SAP's extranet service platform. This platform enables full collaboration between SAP, customers, and partners. The site is segmented into specific portals tailored to the user's needs and provides information about, and access to, SAP services, software, and consulting — with areas dedicated to support, help, education, etc. The site can help users with the evaluation, implementation, and operation of their SAP solutions. SAP Service Marketplace can also help partners and SAP Business One customers with portals created specifically for them. By using Single Sign-On (SSO), SAP Service Marketplace is accessible at any time and from anywhere.

SAP Online Help

SAP provides online help through their SAP Help Portal at *http://help.sap.com/*. The site includes access to extensive documentation from the SAP Library on:

- SAP Solutions
- Service-Oriented Architecture (SOA)
- SAP Business One
- SAP Best Practices
- SAP BusinessObjects

The Help Portal also includes additional information about the documentation, information design at SAP, education services, and links to the SAP Community Network.

SAP Developer Network (SDN) — SAP Community

The SAP Community Network (*http://www.sdn.sap.com*) includes the SDN, Business Process Expert (BPX) Community, University Alliance Community (UAC), and Business Objects Community (BOC), has a diverse and growing membership. SDN, BPX, UAC, and BOC, all provide access to topic threads that will:

- Provide information and training resources to achieve your goals;
- Give you access to the power of true co-innovation.

As an example, the SDN offers deep technical content and expertise for SAP developers, analysts, consultants, and administrators on SAP NetWeaver. SDN members can access a collection of technical content on a range of SAP topics, including expert blogs, technical articles, white papers, how-to guides, moderated forums, software downloads, an extensive E-learning catalog, and a Wiki that supports open communication.

HRExpert

Regardless of company size, Human Resources (HR) is a key function in daily business operations. HRexpert.com provides expert advice and assistance in answering HR-related questions regarding the entire employee lifecycle, including:

- Benefits
- Compensation
- Career development
- Competency mapping
- Employee relations
- Operations
- Performance appraisals
- Recruitment
- Redundancy
- Record keeping

SAP Events and Annual Conferences

ASUG (*http://www.asug.com/Home.aspx*) is the largest community of SAP professionals. Their site maintains a calendar of events (*http://www.asug.com/EventsCalendar/*) that includes annual conferences, BusinessObjects events, virtual events, face-to-face events, volunteer activities, and board of directors meetings available to the international community of SAP users.

User Communities
- **SAP User Groups around the World**

    SAP has a number of international user groups. You can find more information at *http://www.sapusergroups.com/*.

Americas	ASUG Argentina: Argentina *www.sap.com/argentina* ASUG — Associação de Usuários SAP do Brasil: Brazil *www.asug.com.br* ASUG Colombia: Colombia www.asugcolombia.com ASUG Mexico y Centroamérica A.C.: Mexico *www.asug.com.mx* CariSAP: Caribbean *www.carisap.org*
EMEA	SAPience.be: Belgium *www.sapience.be* FSD — Foreningen af SAP brugere i Danmark: Denmark *www.sapfsd.dk* FINUG — SAP Finnish User Group ry: Finland*www.sapfinug.fi* USF — Le club des Utilisateurs SAP Francophones: France *www.usf.fr* DSAG — German-speaking SAP User Group (Deutschsprachige SAP-Anwendergruppe e.V): Germany *www.dsag.de* ISUG — Israeli SAP User Group: Israel *www.isug.org* Aused — GUPS: Italy *www.aused.org* SAP Users Group - Middle East and North Africa (SUG-MENA): Middle East and North Africa *www.sugmena.com* VNSG — Vereniging Nederlandstalige SAP Gebruikers: Netherlands *www.vnsg.nl* SBN — SAP Brukerforening Norge: Norway *www.sap-sbn.no* GUSP: Portugal *www.gusp.com* SUSAP — Slovenian Users of SAP: Slovenia *www.susap.si* AUSAPE — Asociación de Usuarios de SAP de España: Spain *www.ausape.es* SAPSA — SAP Svenska Användarförening: Sweden *www.sapsa.se* SAP UK & Ireland User Group: UK and Ireland *www.sapusers.org*
Asia Pacific	SUGHK — SAP User Group (Hong Kong) Limited: Hong Kong *www.sug.com.hk* INDUS — India User Group of SAP: India *www.induscommunity.com* Japan SAP Users' Group: Japan jsug.org NZSUG — New Zealand SAP User Group: New Zealand *www.nzsug.co.nz* Users of SAP in the Philippines: Philippines Webpage under construction SAP Thai User Group:Thailand

▶ **America's SAP User Group (ASUG)**

ASUG (*http://www.asug.com*) is the largest community of SAP professionals, engaged in helping each other find new and better ways to solve problems and achieve their business goals. ASUG communities (regional chapters and special interest groups (SIGs)) provide opportunities to connect and collaborate with others in the SAP ecosystem based on your job role and interests, industry preferences, or geography. Contact *communities@asug.com* for more information.

▶ **Regional Chapters**

An ASUG chapter is a community of SAP ERP and SAP BusinessObjects professionals in close geographical proximity. Chapter meetings are held for a single day and cover topics of interest as identified by local members. There are 38 geographical locations throughout the United States and Canada.

Alabama	Kentucky	Ohio
Alberta - Western Canada	Maryland - Baltimore	Ontario
Arizona	Michigan	Ottawa
Atlantic Canadian	Midwest - Central	Pacific Northwest
British Columbia	Minnesota	Pennsylvania - Philadelphia
California - Northern	Missouri - St. Louis	Pennsylvania - Pittsburgh
California - Southern	New England	Quebec
Colorado	New Jersey	Texas - Central
Connecticut	New York (Upstate)/ Pennsylvania (Upstate)	Texas - Dallas/Fort Worth
East Tennessee	New York City Metro Area	Texas - Houston
Florida		Utah
Georgia	North Carolina/South Carolina	Wisconsin
Illinois - Chicago		
Indiana	North Carolina/Virginia	

▶ **SIGs**

ASUG SIGs provide members within a specific area of the SAP ecosystem access to networking, education, and support from other SAP professionals with expertise and experience in the areas of process, industry, and technology.

Aerospace & Defense	Data Governance	Business Intelligence Communities (6)
Apparel & Footwear Solution	Development Technologies	BusinessObjects Data Management
Automotive	Integration Technologies and E-Business	Crystal Reports
Business Integration, Technology & Infrastructure (BITI) Communities (10)	Mobile Technologies	Dashboarding
	Security	Emerging Advanced Analytics
Archiving and Information Lifecycle Management	Software Quality Assurance	Enterprise Data Warehousing
	Systems Management	
BusinessObjects Security and Administration	Workflow and Business Process Management	WebI/DeskI (including BusinessObjects Explorer)

Additional Resources

CISUG (Chemical)
Consumer Products
Customer Management Communities (4)
Credit/Accounts Receivable
Customer Service and CRM Service
Order Management
SAP Customer Relationship Management
Enterprise Architecture Communities (3)
Business Process Architecture (BPA)
Enterprise Architecture
SOA (Service Oriented Architecture)
Enterprise Asset Management Community (3)
Capital Projects
MRO Materials and Services
Plant Management
ERP Upgrades
Financial Communities (9)
Asset Accounting
Enterprise Performance Management
FI/CO
Internal Controls
Manufacturing Cost Accounting
Real Estate
Tax
Travel Management
Treasury
Global Banking
Healthcare
High Tech
Human Capital Management (3)

HCM Service Delivery and Workforce Analytics
Talent Management
Workforce Process Management
Media
Mill Products
Mining
Oil & Gas
Pharmaceuticals
Portals Communities (5)
Portal Collaboration, Content Management and Search
Portal Content
Portal Governance and Usability
Portal Implementation and Operational Support
Portal Integration and Interoperability
Product Lifecycle Management Communities (6)
Environmental Health & Safety
New Product Development and Introduction
Product Data Management
Project Centric
Project Systems
Quality Management
Professional Services Providers
Public Sector Communities (3)
Government
Higher Education
K - 12 Education
Rail
Retail
SAP on Sun SIG

Services & Support Communities (5)
Customer Competency Centers/Centers of Excellence
Documentation & Training
Global Implementations
Organizational Change Management
Program Management & Maintenance Strategies
Small & Medium Enterprises Communities (2)
Business One
Small & Medium Enterprise
Solution Manager
Supply Chain Management Communities (9)
Accounts Payable
Distribution and Transportation
Global Trade Services
Inventory and Warehouse Management
Manufacturing
MII
Procurement
Supplier Relationship Management
Supply Chain Planning
Telecommunications
Utilities (3)
Utilities Customer Care and Services
Utilities Power Generation
Utilities Transmission and Distribution
Wholesale Distribution

LinkedIn

Over 75 million professionals use LinkedIn (*http://www.linkedin.com*) to exchange information, ideas, and opportunities, stay informed about their contacts and industry, and find the people or knowledge needed to achieve their goals. A professional network is a valuable asset. Through a professional network you can:

- Find service providers and subject experts who come recommended
- Create and collaborate on projects, gather data, share files, and solve problems
- Gain insights from discussions with like-minded professionals
- Post and distribute job listings to find the best talent for your company

LinkedIn exists to help professionals make productive and successful use of their network. In a globally connected economy, success and competitiveness as a company depends upon faster access to insight and resources.

The Authors

Ajay Jain Bhutoria is a thought leader with over 15 years of experience in consulting and management of global SAP ERP HCM Projects. Ajay is recognized for his deep understanding and appreciation of the customer's business and integration. Ajay has been involved with some of the biggest and complex SAP ERP HCM Global Projects and have successfully led and delivered the transformations providing value to the Customers. Ajay's ability in providing strategic directions to the HR departments, creating roadmaps and designs for high value HR applications and hands-on, functional HR consulting have resulted into satisfied and delighted customers for his consulting firm, Global Business Consulting Services in Fremont, CA.

Cameron Lewis has over 20 years of extensive experience in Human Resources. In his role at Cadence he directs HR's technical staff and systems supporting the primary HR functions and employee lifecycle. His current focus includes defining and implementing a new HR systems strategy emphasizing consolidation, simplification, and security through process re-engineering and the implementation of new/upgraded learning, document, and human capital management solutions.

Index

A

ABAP Dictionary, 36
ABKRS, 36
Absence Quotas, 100, 118
   Infotype 2006, 118
Absences, 107
Absence Type, 102, 104, 206
Access, 242, 246
Accounting Date, 68
Actions, 30
Additional information, 280
Ad hoc query, 282
Adjustment Reason, 50, 60, 61
Administrative functions, 130
Adobe, 218
Adobe interactive form, 224
Anniversaries, 76, 239
Appraisal, 130, 142, 176
   Catalog, 147
   Columns, 140
Appraiser, 134
Approval working time, 204
Architecture, 222
Attachment types, 228, 229
Attendance, 102, 107
Attendance type, 206
Attributes, 194, 276
Audit, 72
   Process, 74
Auditing, 156
Authority, 248
Authorization, 127, 142, 188, 242, 245, 246, 252, 275
Availability, 107

B

Backend objective setting, 146
Background, 175
Background checks, 124, 125
   Open, 125

Bank transfer, 70
Base Salary, 176
Basic insurance coverage, 58
Basic list, 262
Basic pay, 166, 244
Batch Input, 100
Benefit Area, 54
Benefit Elections, 60
Benefit enrollment, 208
Benefit Plan, 56
Benefit programs, 208
Benefits, 50, 52, 54, 56
Benefit salary, 58
Birth certificate, 229
Birthday, 76
Bonus awards, 156
Budget, 161
   Structures, 169
Business rules, 114

C

Calculation Rules, 72
Calibration grid, 180
Career maintenance, 185
Career succession, 184
CATS, 204
Changing, 110
Checking, 248
Chief position, 278
Child roles, 252
Clock-in/clock-out corrections, 206
Collective approval, 204
Column Definition, 177
Column Headers, 176
Column layout, 154
Company properties, 189
Compare talent, 180
Comparing, 252
Comparing appraisal, 134
Compensation budget, 160, 161
Compensation management, 150

Compensation planning, 154, 156, 158, 173
   History, 162
Compensation plans, 164
Compensation process, 174
   Records, 175
Compensation specialist, 168
Compensation statements, 239
Compliance, 38, 252
Comp ratio, 154
Configuration, 280
Contract negotiations, 92
Control, 196
Controlling, 164
Conversions, 278
Copy Benefit Plan, 56
Copying, 56
Correcting, 118
Costs, 56
   Summary, 54
Coverage, 54
Create, 56
   Form scenario, 229
   Ranking, 134
   Record, 24
Currency, 176
Current Payroll Results, 88
Custom, 282
   Field, 44
   Infotype, 28
Customer, 44
Customizing, 142
Custom Messages, 76
Custom transaction, 282

D

Daily Work Schedule, 106
Dashboard, 122, 124, 125
Data, 248
Data Provider, 177
Data Report, 24
Data selection, 234
Deductions, 21
Delete, 66, 74, 82, 88, 162
   Record, 24
Dependent Records, 273
Description, 56

Designing, 150
Design time, 208
Development, 266
Digital personnel file, 236
Directly subordinate, 198
Displaying, 110
   Keys, 280
Divorce, 208
Dynamic selections, 254

E

ECM, 202
Edit, 37, 72
Edit careers, 185
Efficiency, 254
E-learning, 144
Eligibility, 164
Employee, 88, 164, 198, 212, 242
   Data, 234
   Number, 18
   Pay Stubs, 76
   Self-service, 214
Enhancements, 44
Enrollments, 50
Entitlements, 100
Entry, 22
E-recruiting, 124, 125, 127
Error Log Generated, 116
Error messages, 116
ESS, 196, 212
Evaluating appraisal, 134
Exceptions, 164
Export file, 84

F

Factory Calendar, 110
Fast entry, 20, 30
Features, 36
Fields, 52
Files, 84
Filter, 70
Finding, 26
Find Processes, 233
Flexible Spending Account, 50
Focal merit, 150

Focal promotion, 150
Focal Special, 150
Forms, 228
Forms and processes, 218
Functional, 255
Functions, 82

G

Generate, 36, 100
  Internet address, 147
Guided procedures, 208, 209

H

Headcount, 40, 42
Health insurance, 54
Health Plan, 52, 56
Help desk, 284
Hide, 52
Hiring Action, 30
Holiday Calendar, 110
HR
  Activities, 282
  Administrator, 236, 242
  Administrator role, 222, 234, 238
  Master sata, 226
  Tables, 282
  Tasks, 238
HRP1000, 282
HRTMC_PPOC, 185

I

IMG nodes, 280
Improving, 254
Individual appraisal, 146
Information messages, 214
Information system, 255, 260
InfoSets, 262, 268
Infotype, 44, 264, 276
  1003, 44
Infotype 0002
  0003, 68
  0006, 212
Infotype 0008

  0128, 76
  0130, 248
  0168, 58
  0378, 60
  0759, 174
  0760, 164
  1007, 42
  2006, 100
  5008, 144
  Browser, 234
  Characteristics, 29
Input Checks, 105
Insurance, 50
Insurance plan, 61
Integrity, 248
Internal service request, 222
  Scenarios, 223
IT 0000 Actions, 22
iView, 188, 202

J

Job, 184
  Architecture, 184
  Catalog, 184
  Families, 183, 184
Job offer, 18
Job pricing, 171

K

Key performance indicators (KPIs), 122
Key Word Search, 233

L

Language, 272
  Dependent, 272
Launch pad, 202
Layout, 154
Layout Editor, 29
Leave request, 207
Leaving Date, 22
Legal documents, 236
LGMST, 36
Life and work events, 208

Life insurance, 58
Line Editor Commands, 82
List, 36
Locked appraisal, 147
Lock/unlock data records, 235
Logged, 38
Logged Changes, 24, 25
Log-on screen, 284
Long-term incentive, 177
   Awards, 160
Long text, 276
LTI awards, 156

M

Maintain master data, 20
Maintenance, 34
Manager's desk, 202
Managers, 162
Manager self-service, 173, 218, 219
Manual checks, 80
Manually, 278
Marriage, 208
Mass Update, 92
Master data, 94, 188, 242, 280
   Change, 68
MDT, 258
Microsoft Excel, 134
Mini information board, 284
Miscellaneous, 54
Monitoring, 156, 160
   Compensation Budgets, 160
MSS, 198, 202
   Launch pad, 258
Multiple, 198
Multiple employees, 21, 106, 226
Multisource appraisal, 146

N

New appraisal, 130
Nomination status, 182
Notice letter of employee, 229
Notifying, 158

O

Object and Data Provider, 177, 203, 232
Object Manager, 34, 46
Off-cycle, 66
OOSB, 275
Open Enrollment, 60, 61
Organizational changes, 138
Organizational Management, 34, 40
Organizational reassignment, 218
Organizational Structure, 198, 272, 278
Organizational unit, 150, 158, 199, 261, 274
   EE, 47
Org Reassignment Action, 30
Output, 261
OUTWP, 114
Override, 58, 164
   Salary, 58
Overtime, 107
Own data, 244

P

PA30, 20, 26, 276, 280
Paging display, 195
Part appraiser, 138
Pay changes, 222
Pay periods, 76
Payroll, 66
   Area, 63
   Calculations, 110
   Data, 84
   Period, 68
   Result, 74, 81
   Schemas, 82
   Status, 68
   Users, 262
Pay scale, 167
Pay structures, 169
PCRs, 72, 82
Performance, 254
   Appraisals, 142
   Rating, 154
Personal Data, 232
Personal information, 196
Personalize, 259
   Tasks, 193
   View, 193

Index

Personal Work Schedule, 108
Personnel Actions, 30
Personnel administration, 28, 276
Personnel area, 34
Personnel Calculation Rules, 114
Personnel change requests, 218
Personnel Development, 44
Personnel information, 212
Personnel Management, 18
Personnel Number, 18, 26
Personnel Work Schedule, 106
PFCG, 242, 253
PHAP_ADMIN_PA, 130
PHAP_CHANGE_PA, 138
PHAP_CREATE_PA, 147
PHAP_SEARCH_PA, 134
Plan, 56
Planned Compensation, 167
Planned Working Time, 93, 95, 106, 109, 110
Planning Cycle, 160
Planning manager, 158
Planning worksheet, 172
PM01, 28
P_ORGIN, 244
Portal content administration, 188
Portal content directory, 203
Portal roles, 128
Position, 42, 182, 184
Posting Run, 70
P_PERNR, 242, 245
PPOME, 34, 46
P_RCF_ACT, 127
Processes, 66, 182
  Scenarios, 228
Processes and forms, 226
Production, 105, 266
Profiles, 274
Promotions, 222
Providers, 84

Q

Quality, 266
Queries, 254, 268
Quick Search, 26
QuickViewer, 262
Quota overview, 118

R

Ranking, 182
Readiness, 182
Records, 174
Recruiting, 126
  Administrator role, 127
  Team, 122
Recurring payments, 21
Reject, 204
Relationship, 34, 182, 278
Reporting launch pad, 258
Report RHPROFL0, 274
Reports, 238, 258, 266
Requisitions, 122, 126
Restricting, 244
RFC destinations, 252
RPUMKD00, 36
Run Documents, 70

S

Salary changes, 238
Salary increase, 150, 156, 170
Salary surveys, 169
SAP Compensation MSS ECM, 172
SAP GUI, 284
SAP Learning Solution, 144
SAP Query, 262, 266
Schema, 72, 114
SE16, 282
SE61, 284
Search, 46, 198
Search Term Help, 47
Security, 244
Security roles, 252
Settings, 142
Short term, 174
Simple reports, 262
Simplify, 34, 114, 236
Simulation, 66
Single worksheet, 150
SPRO, 280
Staffing Change , 47
Standard Area, 266
Streamline, 208
Structural authorization, 274
Structural display, 260

297

SU53, 246
Sub-schemas, 73
Substitutions, 107
Subtypes, 213
Succession planning, 182
SWDD, 225
System administrator, 130
System messages, 214
System outage messages, 284
System performance, 66

T

T588M, 52
Table PCL2, 88
Table T554S, 103
Talent
   Development, 180
   Group, 122, 183
   Management specialist, 182
   Profiles, 180
   Search iView, 180
Target hours, 204
Task group, 274
Task list, 192
Team calendar, 206
Technical Characteristics, 29
Termination, 62, 198
   Action, 42
   Date, 261
Test environment, 162
Test procedure, 248
Test run, 94
Third Party, 84
Time, 84
Time constraint, 18
Time evaluation, 100, 114, 116 118, 248
Time Infotypes, 107
Time Management, 26, 110
Time recording, 248
Track, 38
Tracking, 24, 40, 156
Training courses, 144
Transaction codes, 34, 146, 280
Transaction SE38, 166
Transferred, 254

Translate, 272
Transport, 266, 278
Troubleshooting, 246

U

Unchecked, 162
Unit, 44
Unlock, 130
Unnecessary columns, 172
Unoccupied, 40
Unpaid leave, 88
Users, 275

V

Vacancy, 40, 42
Vacant, 40
Vacation, 118
Validity period, 138
Visibility, 196

W

WBT, 145
Web application, 214
Weeks certificate, 229
Workbench, 62, 66
Work center, 122, 234
Work contract, 229
Workflow, 131, 218, 227
   Task list, 192
   Template, 206, 274
Working Time, 94, 204
Work schedule, 92, 106, 109, 111 204
Workset, 188
Worksheet, 154

Y

YANA, 81
Year-End Adjustment, 62
YTD calculations, 80

www.sap-press.com

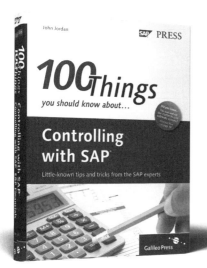

Provides 100 little-known time-saving tips and workarounds for SAP Controlling users, super-users, and consultants

Features a practical, highly-visual, easy-to-use 2-page spread for each topic area

Includes access to a companion e-book or online updates that will be kept current with new tips contributed by readers

John Jordan

100 Things You Should Know About Controlling with SAP

Have you ever spent days trying to figure out how to generate a report in SAP ERP Financials only to find out you just needed to click a few buttons? If so, you'll be delighted with this book — it unlocks the secrets of Controlling in SAP ERP Financials. It provides users and super-users with 100 tips and workarounds you can use to increase productivity, save time, and improve overall ease-of-use of SAP ERP Financials Controlling. The tips have been carefully selected to provide a collection of the best, most useful, and rarest information.

approx. 300 pp., 49,95 Euro / US$ 49.95
ISBN 978-1-59229-341-4, Oct 2010

\>> www.sap-press.com

www.sap-press.com

Provides a complete guide to the functionality of E-Recruiting

Teaches how to configure and use E-Recruiting with other HCM components

Uses a real-world workflow approach

Jeremy Masters, Christos Kotsakis, Venkatesh Krishnamoorthy

E-Recruiting with SAP ERP HCM

This book provides a practical guide to configuring and using SAP E-Recruitment effectively in the real-world. It is written to teach SAP ERP HCM users and implementation teams what the E-Recruiting tool is, so that you can use it effectively in your recruitment process and integrate it easily with other HCM components. Beginning with an overview, the book progresses through the configuration process from a workflow perspective, as used in a real recruiting project. You'll also learn how to integration E-Recruiting with other components.

358 pp., 2010, 69,95 Euro / US$ 69.95
ISBN 978-1-59229-243-1

>> www.sap-press.com

www.sap-press.com

Teaches how to configure ESS and MSS out of the box

Details best practices for customizing ESS and MSS to meet spe-cific business needs

Provides hands-on tips and tricks for deploying self services

Martin Gillet

Configuring and Customizing Employee and Manager Self-Services in SAP ERP

With this detailed guide, you'll find all of the information you need to for customizing Employee Self-Services (ESS), Manager Self-Services (MSS), and the Shared Services Center (SCC). You'll learn everything about the standard "out of the box" configuration, from the early release with ITS services to the latest Web Dynpro offering in ERP 6.0 And with this knowledge, you'll be ready to set up and customize these services to meet your specific business needs.

approx. 400 pp., 69,95 Euro / US$ 69.95
ISBN 978-1-59229-356-8, Feb 2011

>> www.sap-press.com

www.sap-press.com

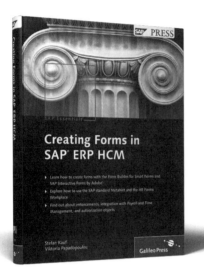

Learn how to present your SAP ERP HCM data effectively

Design remuneration and time statements using Smart Forms and SAP Interactive Forms

Understand the entire process including integration with Payroll and Time Management

Stefan Kauf, Viktoria Papadopoulou

Creating Forms in SAP ERP HCM

This book teaches users how to use the SAP HR Forms Workplace and its Smart Forms and SAP Interactive Forms by Adobe tools to create flexible forms to deliver their HR master data, time data, and payroll results in a professional style. It shows users how to consistently select, conveniently design, and effectively print data from the different sources. It explains how to design remuneration and time statements with both tools, and then how to customize them for specific business requirements. From there it details how to integrate forms with existing applications, including time management and payroll. And it explains form maintenance in HR Forms Workplace, and authorizations in the HR Metadata Workplace. This is the one resource users need to learn how to create and maintain their own HR forms.

229 pp., 2009, 68,– Euro / US$ 85
ISBN 978-1-59229-282-0

>> www.sap-press.com

www.sap-press.com

Provides a completely updated and expanded second edition of this bestselling HR reference

Explains how to meet and perform business requirements with SAP ERP HCM using sample processes

Sven Ringling, Jörg Edinger, Janet McClurg

Mastering HR Management with SAP ERP HCM

This new updated and enhanced edition of the definitive guide to SAP ERP HCM, is written to teach HR managers, functional users, project managers, and others working with HCM about how to use and customize it throughout the entire HR process. From recruiting personnel to transferring HR data to accounting are all covered based on the current release SAP ERP 6.0. This is the one resource the HR team needs to get the most out of their HCM implementation.

664 pp., 2. edition 2009, 69,95 Euro / US$ 69.95
ISBN 978-1-59229-278-3

>> www.sap-press.com

www.sap-press.com

- ✓ Easy and intuitive navigation
- ✓ Bookmarking
- ✓ Searching within the full text of all our books
- ✓ 24/7 access
- ✓ Printing capability

Galileo Press

Interested in reading more?

Please visit our Web site for all
new book releases from SAP PRESS.

www.sap-press.com